STRAIGHT OUT OF HELL 1

WRONG PLACE WRONG TIME

SECOND EDITION

A GUN VIOLENCE SURVIVOR'S STORY

GARRY L. JONES

Copyright © 2016 by Garry L. Jones
(2nd Edition)

All rights reserved. In accordance with the U.S. Copyright Act of 1976, the scanning, uploading, and electronic sharing of any part of this book without permission of the publisher constitute unlawful piracy and theft of the author's intellectual property. If you would like to use material from the book (other than for review purposes), prior written permission must be obtained by contacting the publisher.

Thank you for your support of the author's rights.

VMH™ Publishing

The publisher is not responsible for websites, or social media pages (or their content) related to this publication, that are not owned by the publisher. Quantity sales. Special discounts are available on quantity purchases by corporations, associations, and others. For details, contact the publisher.

Hardback ISBN: 978-0-9979397-2-9

Paperback ISBN: 978-1-9479281-0-7

Author's Note:

The names and characters have been changed to protect the privacy of such individual's. The events documented in this publication are according to the author's memory.

Published in United States of America

10 9 8 7 6 5 4 3 2 1

This book is dedicated in the memory of
Tessie Simmons Jones.

SUNRISE: FEBRUARY 28, 1925   SUNSET: JANUARY 16, 2009

Who was Tessie Jones?

Tessie Jones was a virtuous woman, the matriarch and strength of the Jones family, filled with pride. She took on tremendous responsibility when my grandfather Wesley died. She was a mother, grandmother, aunt, cousin, friend, and neighbor, always willing to help others first, setting her own needs aside.

Tessie Jones was a very loving and humble woman—until you crossed that line. When her family was in danger, she wasn't so kind. Her love was unconditional, and she was very faithful to the church. Who did you call on when others were neglecting God's work? Could that be Tessie Jones?

Tessie Jones cooked a full-course meal each and every day; she knew her children and grandchildren needed energy in order to work and play outside. She also supplied us with spiritual nourishment, and while living in her house, she made sure we attended Sunday School, church, and Vacation Bible School without fail.

Tessie Jones was a strong woman, and whenever sickness put her on her back, she would find the energy to make a great big comeback. No, she didn't tell us she loved us every day, but she expressed her love in a very special way. Is there anyone out there who can follow in her footsteps today?

Tessie Jones, it took me years to understand your character and unique ways. I didn't realize you were laying down the foundation to help the family pave the way for others one day. Could it be that you showed me better than you could tell me? If that's the case, thank you for letting your light shine so the world could see.

Garry L. Jones

TABLE OF CONTENTS

Acknowledgments 1

Dedication 3

CHAPTER 1: Carver Courts 5

CHAPTER 2: The Bonding the Projects Created 7

CHAPTER 3: Big Bad Denderant Jones 11

CHAPTER 4: My Mother's Troubled Past 15

CHAPTER 5: How Doctors Treated Black and White Kids 21

CHAPTER 6: Hustler and Sex in the Hood 25

CHAPTER 7: Gangs in Carver Courts 31

CHAPTER 8: Joining First Baptist Church 35

CHAPTER 9: Carver Courts Christmas 41

CHAPTER 10: Meeting My Father for the First Time 45

CHAPTER 11: The KKK 53

CHAPTER 12: I Was a Devious Kid 59

CHAPTER 13: Legal Hustler 65

CHAPTER 14: Falling Out in the Cucumber Field 71

CHAPTER 15: Carver Courts Socials 73

CHAPTER 16: There Was Something Different About Me 77

CHAPTER 17: Leaving Carver Courts 79

CHAPTER 18: The Trainer 85

CHAPTER 19: My First Real Job 93

CHAPTER 20: My Sport Career Begins 101

CHAPTER 21: Coming into My Own 105

CHAPTER 22: Football and Track Season, 1979 113

CHAPTER 23: High School 119

CHAPTER 24: Heading to North Carolina Central University 127

Chapter 25: Falling in Love Again 139

Chapter 26: He Crossed the Line 147

Chapter 27: The Classic 155

Chapter 28: Classic Memories 159

Chapter 29: Deciding My Major 165

Chapter 30: Getting in a Fight at the University of North Carolina 171

Chapter 31: The Night Coleman Flipped 175

Chapter 32: God Was Warning Me 181

Chapter 33: My Friend Stephon Killed His Girlfriend 189

Chapter 34: God's Warning Came to Fruition 193

Chapter 35: No Justice No Peace 203

Epilogue 207

Where Are they Now 209

Acknowledgements

First and foremost, I would like to thank my Lord and Savior, Jesus Christ; without Him, none of my work would have been possible.

I would like to acknowledge my children: Derrick "Deon" Sutton, LaToya "Nicole" Jones, Malcolm "Keith-Goldwater" Jones, and my daughter-in-law, Sherrie Black Sutton. To my grandchildren, Dereon Sutton and Jada Jones, Dad loves you very much.

I would like to extend my gratitude to the President and Vice President of the Advocate4Justice organization, Vikki Hankins and my brother, Mr. Terry G. Jones. Additionally, I would like to recognize Vikki Hankins for all the hard work she put into my books.

I can't forget my other siblings: Lisa Jones, Duane King, Alicia Rooks, Leslie Nichols Jr., and Kayla Dove; thank you for your continued support.

To all of my good friends, near and far, thank you for your support.

Dedication

I was a senior lieutenant for the Department of Justice, working at the Federal Correctional Institution in Tallahassee, Florida. On April 20, 1999, while making my rounds in the Control Center, I received word at 11:19 a.m. that a shooting had taken place at Columbine High School in Jefferson County, Colorado. From that point until I got off work, I was tuned into the news. Within fifty-two minutes, fifteen students were killed, including both perpetrators, and twenty-one people were injured by gunfire. This shocking event marked a tragic first for schools in the United States and became known as the Columbine High School Massacre.

Fifteen years later, as a retired lieutenant from the Department of Justice, I faced another heartbreak on February 14, 2018. My wife and I were out enjoying lunch for Valentine's Day. Upon returning home, we turned on the television, only to discover that seventeen people were dead following a shooting at Marjory Stoneman Douglas High School in Parkland, near Fort Lauderdale, Florida. This tragedy is now referred to as the Parkland Massacre.

Since the Columbine High School Massacre in 1999, there have been twenty-five active shootings at schools in America. Yes, the United States of America—the best country in the world—cannot safeguard our children at home, yet we can go overseas to war and protect other people's kids. This is a travesty, as the majority of our House of Representatives is funded by the National Rifle Association, and the laws being created are not helping our citizens stay safe. The weapon that can inflict the most damage in the shortest amount of time is the AR-15, which is legal to own in the U.S. This dangerous weapon should be outlawed, except in circumstances such as fighting in a war, during a riot, or in other disturbances.

Our children should be looking forward to attending their senior prom, going to college, graduating, serving in the military, starting regular jobs, becoming lawyers, doctors, engineers, or politicians, and dreaming of getting married and having children. Instead, they are marked by injuries, disability, and death. If children do not receive proper help after a traumatic experience, they risk suffering from post-traumatic stress disorder.

This book is dedicated to anyone who has been a victim of gun violence but chose to be a survivor. Families who have lost loved ones to gun violence will forever be in my prayers. May God continue to grant those families the much-needed peace to live productive lives.

CHAPTER 1

Carver Courts

Front Row Left to Right, Uncle John Jones, Grandmother Tessie Jones and Uncle Earl Jones - Second Row Left to Right, Cousin Annie Mae Grimes, Aunt Mamie Johnson, Denderant Jones, Aunt Arnetta Dixon, Mother Vergie Chalmers, Aunt Mary Mason, and Aunt Mavis Jones (My Family)

The projects where I grew up produced lawyers, doctors, musicians, teachers, and a judge. Very successful people come from the projects or low-income housing. My Uncle Jay was teaching and still living in the household (the projects); my Aunt Denderant, a guidance counselor, lived in our household (the projects); my Uncle Hamm worked at one of the top-paying jobs in Kinston while living in the household in the projects.

In my opinion, people continued to live there because they were trying to help their parents out. Another reason was that it wasn't easy for a Black person to get a house unless they had pretty good credit and a lot of money for a down payment. Most Black people could afford a mortgage; it was the high down payment and the credit that held them back.

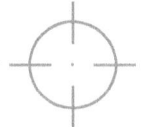

CHAPTER 2

The Bonding the Projects Created

It was the bond that each family had. The one thing that connected family members. It's not like the projects today, where you can't trust each other. The way the projects used to be back then, if your child did something wrong and another adult found out, that adult would whip your ass, and when you got home, you had another ass whipping coming.

It was all about family ties. Our neighborhood was a family-oriented society. We had a community. Carver Courts and the surrounding projects—like Richard Green, Simon Bright, Mitchell Wooten, and Holloway Courts—were communities within themselves.

As a matter of fact, we didn't consider our community a project because it didn't look like the typical projects up North, in the Midwest, or in other Western states.

*Me on the Outside of Our Home in the Projects
(Carver Courts)*

When they say «projects,» you think of high-rise, poverty-stricken housing and ghetto-type places. As a matter of fact, we didn't live in a high rise. We lived in what you might call townhouses or something similar. I mean, if you think about it, we had an upstairs with three to four bedrooms, a downstairs with a living room and a kitchen, and believe it or not, we had a pantry.

I'm not ashamed of where I came from because if it weren't for the projects, I wouldn't be the man I am today. I'm a strong family man with good old-fashioned family values. That means I knew how to take care of my responsibilities and to be responsible for my actions and their consequences.

My Uncle Jay was the man of the house. My grandmother and the rest of my aunts, along with Jay, helped raise me. Growing up, I saw what was going on—my mother left to go stay in D.C.; she was young and wild. She was out there in the streets, and my father didn't spend that much time with us. So, Jay, being the man that he is, became the father figure.

My Aunt Denderant used to say that neither my father nor my mother wanted us, and that my brother and I needed to bond instead of fighting because we only had each other. "You all don't have anyone but each other" were her harsh words, but Jay took another approach. Instead of adding fuel to the fire, he kept his comments to himself in reference to my father. Jay's attitude was, "My sister left the children on his mother," so he decided to help raise us to take the stress off my grandmother.

As I got older, Jay realized that I loved sports, but he wanted me to also be involved in getting a good education. He knew I could go a long way with education, but at the same time, he was a teacher and, at one time, he was an All-American quarterback in college. Jay understood that things had to be put in their proper perspective. He was that strong, positive male role model that most kids are lacking today.

Jay was the first person who made me realize that in order to live in this world and be successful, you had to read! He emphasized reading educational stuff, not just *Sports Illustrated*, *Jet Magazine,* or *Ebony.* He wanted me to read positive things—things that were going to help me in life; I couldn't see it back then. I didn't want to see it back then because I didn't like to read. He told me to read something every day.

I hated reading. My comprehension skills were average because I didn't read a lot. It's ironic because whenever I read something I liked, I could recite everything I had just read, but when it came to something I didn't like, I couldn't recite a damn thing. It's amazing how the mind works. I remember Jay taking me with him when he went to Fayetteville, North Carolina. He was going to pick up a stereo set, and while we were riding, he would point out the signs on the highway and explain to me what the signs meant: signs such as "railroad crossing," "slippery when wet," "one-way streets," "slow down when coming around a curve," and other highway signs.

I was about ten years old. He was teaching me about the signs on the highway; in reality, he was teaching me how important it was to know how to read. Jay was trying to instill in me that success depended on your ability to read. I appreciate him because now I realize that he was a significant part of my life; my aunts, my grandmother, and my other Uncle Hamm played significant roles in the overall success of my life as well.

CHAPTER 3

Big Bad Denderant Jones

My Aunt Denderant Jones was a complete hell-raiser, a no-nonsense type of woman. She was the type of aunt that loved you but wouldn't show it. It was hard to comprehend her love. If you looked at her wrong, she would fuss you out, and she's still that way today. Everyone in the projects knew she didn't play. I guess her love was tough love, but her love damn near drove me crazy.

She would give me money or buy me things, and when I would ask her a question, she would start fussing. I guess the pressure was getting to her as well, having to raise her nephews and nieces. I love my mother, even though she wasn't there, but my mother's lack of raising us put a lot of pressure on her siblings.

My aunts and uncles had to give up a lot of things because food and clothes had to go towards feeding the nephews and nieces. Not only did my grandmother make sure we got everything we needed, but my uncles and aunts played a major role in giving us things that my grandmother couldn't provide. My grandmother's oldest children, Mamie (Jean), Arnetta, and Mary, were staying up north and they contributed as well.

I came to realize why my Aunt Denderant was a no-nonsense type of woman. Denderant became irritated because it was her sister who was out there having these babies, not her. My mother was gone and expected my grandmother to raise these babies.

Denderant was one of those aunts that you had to grow to love. She treated my friends like shit; whenever I would have company, she would tell them, "Take your stinky tails home and don't come back." Denderant was the type of person that when she told you to do something, you better do it. I don't give a damn if you were sleeping, doing cartwheels, flips, or whatever; if you didn't do your chores around the house, she would come on the basketball court in front of your friends and embarrass the hell out of you.

I remember one time we were on the basketball court playing an official game— Carver Courts against Richard Green. We were playing a serious game, and Roland Tate was refereeing. They had tables out on the basketball court, and people were keeping score. You know that was the thing around summertime, playing basketball. Denderant came out there, "You bring your butt home right now! I said bring your butt home right now and empty this trash."

This shit was embarrassing; even the fellows were afraid of her. When my cousins Brian Johnson, Curtis Johnson, Cedric Dixon, Garrick Dixon, and my cousin Sharon Mason came from up north, they would fall up under Dender's raft. What Dender said went—no questions asked.

Dender's other sister, Mavis (Colleen), took a different approach. She wasn't mean like Denderant, but if you left the house without being well-groomed, she would come and get you, then comb your hair and make sure you didn't go back outside until you looked decent.

My mother had four children by the age of eighteen: me, Pete, Lisa, and Jr., and we were all raised in the same household. My brother Jr. would later go stay with his father in Texas. When my sister Lisa was in the 9th grade, she got out of hand and would later leave North Carolina to stay with my mother in Washington, D.C., even though her stay was short. After one year with my mother, Lisa would join her brother Jr. in Texas.

I must admit, when I got older, I didn't realize that my grandmother's two youngest children weren't that much older than me and my brother Pete.

Today, Denderant is still a no-nonsense woman, but she gives us anything we want; she even helps me out with my kids, as does my Aunt Mavis.

Later on in life, my Aunt Dender had a son of her own. His name was Larry Burney Jr. (L.B., L-Mak, The Bisel to the Diesel). L.B. is her pride and joy, and after having him, life became easy for everyone— but only for a short period of time. Therefore, I am grateful and appreciative that my grandmother had that much love for her daughter (my mother) that she kept us and gave us a great life.

CHAPTER 4

My Mother's Troubled Past

My Birth Certificate – I Was Born in a Backroom

I t's hard to go into details about my mother. If I'm not mistaken, my mother had all of her kids in Carver Courts, with the exception of my brother Jr. What I'm trying to say is she had all of her kids early. She was a young mother and didn't take care of us; our grandmother, aunts, and uncles took on this responsibility. I don't hold this against her because we had everything we needed as kids, but there were times I used to wonder what type of kid I would have been if I had been raised by my mother.

My mama dropped out of high school probably at the age of sixteen—I think at the time a person couldn't drop out of school unless they were sixteen years old.

She got married to this dude named Keith, who is Jr.'s father. Keith was stationed at Camp Lejeune in Jacksonville, North Carolina. She never married my father; she married Keith. She met him in Kinston. Our hometown, Kinston, is where a lot of Marines used to come and pick up women. I guess Keith swept her off her feet and they got married.

After they got married, she moved on base with him. My siblings and I used to go on base and stay for a little while, but my grandfather found out there was some fighting in front of us, so he didn't allow us to go back on base. He didn't want his grandchildren to witness the violent relationship my mother and Keith had. The only thing I can remember about Camp Lejeune was that my brother and I had our tonsils taken out. Before my grandfather died, he made my grandmother promise him on his deathbed. This was in the year 1970. He told my grandmother to make sure she raised me and my brother Pete. He also told her that she was probably going to have trouble with my sister Lisa, but not to let the grand boys out of her sight.

My grandmother fulfilled my grandfather's dream. My grandmother was a strong Black woman, even though she was high yellow, damn near looking white, but I loved the hell out of her. I was going through some photos and saw my great-grandmother; I didn't know she was part Indian, and my great-grandfather was very dark-skinned.

When my grandmother told you to do something, she meant it, and this lady would fuss all the time. I think this is where Denderant got all of her fussing from. My grandmother would always talk about how she was raised. Even though she was the youngest of nine children, she would often talk about how they lived on a farm, and she was just as strong as her older sisters and brothers. When she would talk about this, she would always have a smile on her face. I believed my grandmother when she said she was just as strong as her brothers and sisters because whenever we got in trouble, my grandmother would knock you to "summerset." Summerset was a place unknown and unheard of. My grandmother was the type of woman who loved her grandchildren. She allowed us to make some mistakes and encouraged us to be ourselves. But when our behavior got out of hand and we started talking back, she would hit us with a backhand and we'd land on the floor. We could get away with almost anything except talking back, and she made sure we addressed her as "Yes, ma'am."

As we got older and the children started getting out of hand, that's when my Uncle Jay would instill the discipline. Can you imagine going to school where your uncle was the teacher and, at home, he was the disciplinarian? My siblings and I couldn't act up in school because the teachers knew Jay was our uncle, and as soon as we got in trouble, we would be sent to Jay's room, only to get a paddling in the hallway. It didn't stop there; we got our butts torn out of the frame when we got home.

My grandmother knew if I got into trouble in school, someone had to provoke me, so she didn't just take that person's side. The teachers used to send my report card home with an unsatisfactory note about my conduct. My grandmother didn't believe everything that a teacher said about her grandchildren, especially me. If the teachers wrote a note about my sister Lisa's conduct, she was more likely to believe the teacher. It was very rare that my brother Pete got bad conduct. Pete was slick; he never showed his trump card. If you said anything about Pete, my grandmother would turn a deaf ear.

I can remember one incident about my brother that shocked my grandmother. It was during Christmas time. My grandmother used to always have some homemade wine that she had gotten from someone in the country. The wine always stayed in the closet. This particular night, Pete was going in the kitchen closet from the living room, but he would always exit through the kitchen door instead of coming back through the living room. He did this about three times.

Grandmother got up to see why Pete kept coming into the kitchen. She looked in the closet and realized the wine she had was getting low. Of course, my grandmother didn't drink. My grandmother got suspicious and went through the kitchen door to the outside of the house, and that's when she saw my brother with a jar of wine in it. Pete was stealing the wine and giving it to Shellcat and the boys.

My grandmother was shocked because she never would have thought Pete would be stealing—or should I say taking—

the wine and giving it away. This type of behavior was expected of me, but not Pete. I didn't drink at all; as a matter of fact, I didn't drink my first beer until I graduated from high school. My brother Pete doesn't drink alcohol at all.

My grandmother would allow my aunts and uncles to discipline us, but she didn't allow them to go too far. If she felt like the punishment didn't fit the action taken by my uncles and aunts, my grandmother would overturn their punishment and drop it down to a lesser punishment. What I'm trying to say is, if we were getting ready to get corporal punishment for something minor, my grandmother would step in and say, "No whipping today; the children just won't go outside to play."

She tried not to ever overrule Denderant or Jay; she knew they were trying to raise us to do the right thing, and in that sense, she never overruled them. She took care of me and spoiled me because I was a real sick growing up. I had ulcers, asthma, and the secret disease called depression. I was this pitiful little boy.

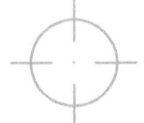

CHAPTER 5

How Doctors Treated Black and White Kids

When I used to have asthma attacks, the doctors would prescribe this bad-tasting medication that made me vomit. They didn't give Black children samples of the new medications. When they prescribed medication for Black kids to take, if it didn't work, they would write another prescription. If the second prescription didn't work, you'd go back and get a shot in your arm. My grandmother wasn't making much money, and all her money went towards my medication.

Sometimes, I felt like a burden to the family because I was sick a lot, and most of the time my grandmother would have to take off work to take me to the doctor. It wasn't until I got older that I realized white doctors treated white children differently than Black children when it came to medical care.

When my daughter was born, she was born with asthma. I remember the first time she had an asthma attack; I took her to the hospital, and a Black doctor treated her by giving her a nebulizer and a mask to breathe in the medication. This is where you put some liquid medication into the machine and breathe it in as not to cause you to vomit.

I told the doctor, "This must be some new technology?" "No," he said, "these machines have been around ever since the '60s." I thought to myself, I was born in 1964, and when I was small, I stayed in the doctor's office taking that bullshit medication and buying Primatene mist off the counter. Why didn't the doctor prescribe me a nebulizer, knowing that I had a weak stomach, and why didn't they prescribe me inhalers to prevent me from having asthma attacks? I remember being in school and seeing white children with inhalers, but the inhalers weren't Primatene mist.

These thoughts didn't come to my mind until I took my daughter to the hospital. All of those years I suffered, and the doctors didn't provide me with the best medical care. Whether my grandmother could have afforded it or not, she wasn't given the option.

The medication they gave me took two to three hours to take effect, but the white children had the opportunity to feel good right away because they were given the best medical care. Whenever I go to the doctors now and they write me a prescription, I ask them to give me a sample—if the sample medication works, only then will I get the prescription filled. These companies give the doctors samples to promote their medication, and the doctors give them to the rich people who can afford their medication and say the hell with the poor people. They don't offer them samples.

Things have improved now, but in order for things to improve further, you have to demand that they improve by opening your mouth and asking questions. I know there is no cure for asthma, but if you receive good medical care for your asthma, you will feel a lot better. As much money as my grandmother spent on medication for me, she could have moved out of the projects years before she actually moved.

I remember being in the doctor's office one day, waiting for them to call me in for my appointment. I picked up a magazine and started to read an article about prescriptions. I read that the pharmaceutical companies send doctors and their families on paid vacations if they write a lot of prescriptions to their patients and get the prescriptions filled at certain pharmacies.

If you lived in a small town with only one or two drug stores, you didn't have a choice but to get your prescription filled there. The doctors and the pharmaceutical companies work hand in hand, meaning, "If you send me business, I will send your family on a paid vacation."

CHAPTER 6

Hustler and Sex in the Hood

In every project, there are always going to be hustlers and number rackets going on—Carver Courts was no different. My best friend's mother used to run the numbers; they call it playing the lotto these days. As a matter of fact, she wasn't the only one running numbers; I can name at least eight people in the projects that I know ran the numbers, but I'm not going to name them because they might still be doing it.

Everyone played the numbers, even the people who were supposed to 'serve and protect' (the police). I used to love going to my best friend's house because his mother played a card game called spades, and she was good at it. She was a multi-tasked woman, meaning she could do a lot of things at one time. She would play spades while holding one of her infants in one arm, deal the cards with her free hand, and smoke a cigarette all at the same time. When her infant child would start crying, she would take out her breast and start feeding her. That was the first time I considered being exposed to a breast.

While she was still playing spades, people would come over to the house and put their numbers in. She would give them a receipt and let them know she was playing cards, then turn around and tell the people who were playing spades, "It's your turn to deal the cards." She did all of this without missing a beat. Anytime you played spades with Cookie, you better know how to play, because if you didn't, you were going to get scolded. She and Roland Tate were the only ones who would scold you if you didn't know how to play. They took the game of spades seriously. Mind you, I was nine or ten years old playing spades with adults, but Roland and Cookie didn't give a damn—they looked at you as an adult if you were their spade partner.

I reneged a couple of times when I played spades. To renege means to go back on one's word or promise, but when you renege in playing cards, it means to play a card that is not of the same suit led when one can follow suit. For example, for the people who don't know anything about spades—if the other team played a club, and you played a spade card to cut the team's hand (book) to win, and later on during the game, when the other team played a club and you played a club, that is called 'reneging.' Once the other team discovered you reneged, they are obligated to take three of the books that you had won.

The taking of the three books can cause the other team to be set and lose the game. Take, for another example, if a team said that they could win five books and they made their five books, but the other team discovered you reneged, they would take three of your books, which would leave you with only two books at the end of the game, and then you lose points. Cookie would say after you made a mistake, "You shouldn't have sat your little ass at the table if you didn't know how to play spades." She would then make you get up from the table to replace you with a more experienced spade player.

Roland would start stuttering when trying to explain to you how you messed up while smoking his pipe and blowing smoke in your face all at the same time. The other fellows would laugh at you. Living in the hood, you got schooled very fast. Later on, Mr. Parrot would come around and collect his money. Mr. Parrot was the gangster who lived above the café, or as the old-school people called it, 'Harlem's Inn.'

This place was an eatery run by Mr. Fuller at the time. You could tell Mr. Parrot was a gangster; he used to dress in a suit, shirt, tie, and matching shoes. A lot of women used to come out of Mr. Parrot's apartment. I think they were his prostitutes, giving him his money. After Mr. Parrot received his money, he would give my best friend's mother her cut. She would then smile and ask, "Does anyone want to play Pokeno?"

This was a game that was played for money. Several cups were put on the table, labeled as corners, center, diagonal, four of a kind, and Pokeno. Before the game started, everyone who played had to put money in each one of those cups. Some people who were low on money often cheated until they were caught. It was rare that anyone could get over on my best friend's mother; she had an eye like an eagle.

This game was played with cards, and whenever the right card landed your way, you could claim one of the cups with money in them. But the game stops when someone says "Pokeno"—

meaning they won. Of course, my best friend's mother would get her cut because the game was being played at her house.

Whenever the guys wanted to watch X-rated movies, an older friend of mine would show them at his house, but you had to pay ten cents to come in. Whenever his mother would leave to go to work in the summertime, he would invite the boys over. This guy was about five years older than I, but my Aunt Denderant and his sister were pretty good friends. Denderant didn't know this was going on, but anyway, this guy would show the X-rated films with one of those old library projectors—the machine where you had to put the film inside this gadget and turn it on to view the picture. He didn't have a screen, so he just used the wall in the pantry to project the film. I used to get an eye full. If anyone in my family had any clue this was going on, I would still be on punishment today. I would have gotten a whipping first, then placed on punishment.

Needless to say, this man went into the military. It is my understanding that he is now retired. There were also some perverts in the hood. When I was playing in the recreational center, this older, light-skinned Vietnamese guy touched my sister on the butt. Lisa couldn't have been no more than ten years old. I ran out of the center to tell my Uncle Jay. Jay was a teacher at the time, and normally, Jay is laid back. He always quelled volatile situations, but this time, Jay made all the kids get out of the center.

What happened next surprised me. Jay moved all the ping pong tables, pool tables, and chairs to the corner of the room and challenged the Vietnamese guy to come into the center of the room because he was going to give this guy a good old Carver

Courts ass whipping for touching his niece on the butt. Jay balled up his fist—his eyes were red as fire. All the kids that Jay made leave the center climbed onto the window of the center just to see the big fight. They were all disappointed because the Vietnamese guy refused to fight Jay.

It was good that Jay didn't fight the guy because Jay was a school teacher. Maybe the reason why he didn't push the issue was that he could see the kids looking through the window. Jay was a role model, and this would have set a bad example for a teacher to be fighting, but he had every right to whip that guy's butt. It bothers me when I hear about children being touched inappropriately by an adult. I think about what that Vietnamese did to my sister. I always taught my children that if an adult touches them in their private area, they should make sure to come home and tell me. I would have whipped that guy's butt myself, but Jay made me leave the center as well.

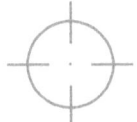

CHAPTER 7

Gangs in Carver Courts

In the early 1970s, we had gangs in Carver Courts, but the purpose of the gangs was to look after the community. We didn't go around shooting and stabbing people or doing any and all types of drive-bys. We fought with our hands.

In my studies, I came to understand that the purpose of gangs was to protect the community by making sure no one came into the neighborhood to destroy it. The gangs that exist today are totally different. They are cowards! Destroying property and taking human lives in your neighborhood is downright foolish; to say the least, it is stupid. If you have to kill someone to be accepted into a gang, then you don't need that gang. Breaking the law is not cool, and if you think so, your mind is distorted. You are committing genocide of your own race.

We created a gang in Carver Courts called the Dog Team. We marched around the whole neighborhood calling cadence: D-O-G-T-E-A-M, Dog Team. The entire neighborhood would stand outside and be in awe of us. We were in tune with who we were; we didn't need anyone to tell us who we were. We were a part of something good; we motivated ourselves.

My Uncle Steve Mason came down from Washington, D.C. to reside and opened up a convenience store called 'Steve's Grocery.' Steve was married to my Aunt Mary. Uncle Steve was what some people might call radical. I think he may have marched back in the '60s with the Black Panthers because I saw a photo of him with Angela Davis. Most people use "radical" in a negative connotation, but radical is a person who advocates fundamental political, economic, and social reforms by direct and often uncompromising methods. In other words, he fought for what he believed in.

He created an organization called 'Steve's Army.' If we wanted to join, he ordered us military uniforms and taught us about respecting one another as well as our neighbors. We started off as officers, and then if we did something good, we were promoted to corporal, sergeant, captain, and general. We had to keep our grades up in order to be in Steve's Army. We had to be well-groomed and know how to march in unison. I remember when I got my first set of green fatigues with my black army boots; I had to salute and stand at attention. That was a good feeling. We were disciplined young men. The highest rank I achieved was general. Steve also taught me how to box.

Steve used to wear his Dashiki; he was pro-Black, but this didn't mean that he was anti-white. I also had another uncle who was pro-military: my Uncle Victor Johnson. He taught me a lot as well. Vic was cool, and he married my Aunt Mamie (Jean).

I would be lying if I said there weren't any fights in Carver Courts because there were. Two of my friends, Roscoe and

Andre, got into arguments over playing cards or shooting pool; I can't exactly remember which one they fought over, but I do remember Roscoe body slamming Andre on the ground. "Don't be there when I come back!" This is what Andre told Roscoe when he got up off the ground.

Roscoe didn't run from anyone, but everyone knew if Andre said he was coming back, then more than likely Andre was coming back with something in his hands. A few minutes later, Andre came back, and he and Roscoe started fighting again. Andre took out a butcher knife and stabbed Roscoe in the chest. Roscoe started running away from Andre because Andre kept swinging the knife, but the more Roscoe ran, the weaker he became; Andre was running behind him, trying to keep stabbing him.

If it wasn't for Antonio Jenkins catching up with Andre and grabbing him, Andre probably would have stabbed Roscoe again. When Roscoe got home, the ambulance was called, and Roscoe was rushed to the hospital. Roscoe almost died because the stab wound was an inch away from his heart.

From time to time, you'd hear about someone being killed in Carver Courts, but it's nothing like the killings that go on today in the projects. One morning, I woke up only to find out that someone was killed in my neighborhood—not with a gun but with a bat. Two guys were fighting, and one guy picked up a bat and hit the other guy in the head. His brains were in the ball cap he was wearing. This happened just two feet away in my yard. Things like this happened far and in between. It was rare to hear about something like this, but today, it's rare if you don't hear about something of this nature taking place in the hood.

My best friend's sister Cynthia (Cymp Juan) was fighting a guy in Carver Courts (by the way, we were 'puppy lovers'). The guy, who was younger than her, cut her in the face because he couldn't fight like a man. He wanted to act tough, but he couldn't fight unless he had a weapon. He cut her with one of those knives called a hawk knife, and he was only eleven years old. Why would a person so young carry a hawk knife?

I must say Cynthia was beating the hell out of the guy, and he was embarrassed. If I'm not mistaken, he went home to get the knife. She was a tough girl; she always held her own, and today, she is still holding her own.

All of Mrs. Christine's children held their own, but when her children got in trouble, she would whip them with one of those orange racing rod tracks. She was a strict disciplinarian— all of the mothers in Carver Courts that I knew were strict disciplinarians. Mothers like Mrs. Sue, Mrs. Willie Jay, Mrs. Dot Smith, Mrs. Esther Bell, Mrs. Neat Parker, Mrs. Hilda Williams, Mrs. Mattie Jacobs, Mrs. Letha Mae Sutton, Mrs. Swannie Irving, and the list goes on.

CHAPTER 8

Joining First Baptist Church

First Baptist Church was located across the street from Carver Courts. Most of the people who lived in Carver Courts attended this church. From the time I was about seven years old, my siblings and I started going to First Baptist. My grandmother would always take us to her church out in the country called King's Chapel Church. I can't recall why we stopped going out into the country to attend church, but whatever the reason, I wasn't disappointed (my grandmother continued attending the church in the country).

Initially, I wasn't happy about going to church, but when my siblings and I went, we had fun. I remember my first Sunday School teacher, Mrs. Bannerman; I think we attended her class because of the age difference. After leaving Mrs. Bannerman's class, I started attending Mrs. Burney's class. She was a lot older, but she was very, very nice. Mrs. Burney always had snacks for us when we attended her class. We would always cut up in Mrs. Burney's class, but for some reason, she regained control very quickly by asking us to read scriptures from the Sunday School books. Another reason I liked attending Mrs. Burney's class was that it was upstairs near the balcony. We always had a contest in church or Sunday School. It was all about competition, and I loved competition. Mrs. Burney's class would either win the attendance banner or the offering banner. We always wanted to outdo the other classes.

I think Mrs. Bannerman's son was the superintendent of Sunday School, and my brother Pete or my best friend Antray was the assistant superintendent. Whenever our class would win a banner, it would be announced, and we had to stand up and be recognized. After Sunday School, we had to attend church, which wasn't fun at all.

The only thing fun about church was when the Holy Ghost got into some of the members, and they would start running all over the church shouting. My friends and I would look at each other and burst out laughing. Of course, we didn't understand what was going on. We were just kids. As a matter of fact, I thought First Baptist was my church home because I attended the church and thought I was paying my tithes when I put a dime in the offering plate as it went around.

I had no clue that in order to belong to a church, you had to first join it. I could never figure out why some people were putting money in envelopes instead of just dropping their money in the plate as it was passed around. This confused me.

My play sister, Francis Irving, and I had a conversation about this.

"Gold, you are not a member of the church," she stated.

"First Baptist is my church!" I said, confused.

"You are still not a member," she replied.

Of course, back then, I didn't know what a member was. I always felt if I attended a church, then that was my church.

Me Standing in Front of the 'Old' First Baptist Church
(A Portion of Church is Seen in Background)

"No, Gold, you have to join the church," she said. Then she explained, "After the pastor preaches his sermon, he makes an announcement for everyone who desires to be part of the First Baptist Church family to come up front and do whatever the church does to make you a member."

When I got older and started to learn more about the church, that's when I decided to make my move to join.

One Sunday, Fran asked me, "Are you going to join the church?"

"Yes, but I don't want to be saved."

"You don't have to be saved just because you joined."

"Well, why is it that when the people walk down the aisle, the pastor saves them?"

She said, "Look boy! They give you an opportunity to be a member of the church or to give your life to Christ; it's your choice."

"I still don't want to be saved. I want to wait until I get older to be saved; that's what old people do; they are the saved people."

I remember it like it was yesterday; Pastor Raynor, the pastor of First Baptist Church, had just finished giving his sermon, and he made that famous announcement, "If you would like to join the church, come up front." Of course, when you go up front, they have a chair waiting for you to sit in. The questions the pastor usually asks are, "Do you want to join the church or do you want to give your life to Christ?"

He used to say, "While the blood is still running warm in your veins, you still have a chance to give your life to Christ."

I told the people who surrounded me that I wanted to join the church, but I didn't want to give my life to Christ. After I joined, all the members of the church came around and gave me the "right hand of fellowship." To this day, I don't have a clue what the "right hand of fellowship" was all about. I just knew everyone shook my hand. I can't recall whether they shook my left or right hand. The pastor announced that baptism would be the following week.

When the next week came, my grandmother took me to church on a Saturday to be baptized. I was nervous, and I just wanted to get it over with. I was told to go in the back with the deacons of the church to change clothes. I was nervous about that as well; I didn't need anyone to come with me to change clothes. I was sixteen years old; I knew how to take my clothes off.

After coming from the back of the church to the front, Reverend Raynor was already in the pool of water, and he motioned for me to come in. I hesitated and looked at my grandmother; of course, she didn't show any emotions. When I stepped into the pool of water, the pastor did what pastors do and prayed; before I knew it, my head was under the water so fast that I panicked when he brought me up. I was coughing and trying to get the water out of my eyes. What struck me the most was when he said, "All of your sins were washed away and now you are a child of God." Those weren't his exact words, but I knew what he meant.

I got out of the pool and went to the back of the church to dry off. I changed clothes and went over to my grandmother, telling her that he saved me and I didn't want to be saved until I got old. This was supposed to be a baptism; he wasn't supposed to make me born again. My grandmother looked at me and said, "Let's go."

I guess her mindset was, "This boy doesn't have a clue about anything related to the church." When I became older, I realized that you can be in the church, but that doesn't mean you know anything about the church. I always prided myself on not getting caught up in the "politics" of the church.

What I mean by this is, so many people want to get close to the pastor, and they want to be buddy-buddy with him as if they are trying to gain some brownie points. I never understood this to this day. What I do know is that in order to go further in your spiritual life, you must study the word, participate in Bible studies, and go to church. This doesn't mean that you have to be at the church before the doors open.

If you have a family, there has to be a balance. You can't neglect your family or your duties at home, whether you are a male or female spouse, just because all your time is spent at the church.

CHAPTER 9

Carver Courts Christmas

First Row Sister Lisa, Brother Leslie, and, of Course Me Second Row Cousin Annie Mae Grimes, and Brother Pete During Christmas

I loved Christmas time in Carver Courts. Like I said earlier, we were a tight-knit community, and during Christmas, we were even tighter. I could always feel the Christmas spirit. It was a wonderful feeling.

Our family was popular in Carver Courts, and we always had a lot of company over at the house. My friends used to come over and say, "Man, how did you all get so many presents under that tree?" The presents we had under the tree came almost to the top; that's how many presents we had. My brother and I had at least fifteen presents each. Whatever we wanted for Christmas, we would get.

Our aunts and uncles would ask us what we wanted for Christmas, and we would tell them. They would say, "You all can't get that stuff for Christmas; you all want too much."

My Aunt Denderant would say, "You all are not going to get more than three things for Christmas; who do you think you are? People don't have that type of money to get you all that stuff; you better go get a job."

Denderant knew damn well we weren't old enough to work. My Aunt Mavis (Colleen) would always play her 45 (single), and the Christmas record she played the most was "Please Come Home for Christmas" by Charles Brown.

My cousin Evelyn loved listening to this sad Christmas song called "What Do the Lonely Do at Christmas" by The Emotions. I never went without getting my grandmother a gift; I would sell some bottles and go down to Gibb's Supermarket to buy her four kitchen glasses that cost $1.00. I was never to be outdone.

I would get my cousin Annie Mae to wrap my grandmother's gift because if it were up to me, I would have just given it to her on Christmas without any wrapping paper. Annie Mae would always say, "You didn't take the price tag off." None of that mattered to me.

"You know you have to go to bed early because Santa Claus and his reindeers are not going to stop by the house until you go to sleep. But you can go outside and look in the sky and see his reindeers," is what my Aunt Mavis and Aunt Denderant used to say.

For some strange reason, I never saw Santa Claus riding with his reindeers, and when I would go back in the house and tell my aunts, they would say, "You must have just missed him because we saw him earlier. Go upstairs and go to sleep; he's not coming by until you go to sleep."

The next day when Pete, my sister Lisa, and I came downstairs, we tore through our presents looking to see what we had gotten. The very things Denderant said we weren't going to get, we got those things plus more. We had it going on. Our Aunt Arnetta, Mamie, and Mary would always send their presents from up north. Pete and I were the first kids to have an Air Hockey table—Air Hockey was expensive.

We all had bikes, and some kids in the neighborhood only got a bike for Christmas, but we had fifteen times the gifts than anyone else. I loved my Rock 'Em Sock 'Em Robots, and all the kids would come over to play at our house until it got really late.

Denderant would say, "You need to take your stinky tails home now and play with your own toys." None of my friends got mad at Denderant because they knew she talked like that. My Uncle Jay and Larry would stay up all night putting most of our toys together, and I guess my father came over in the middle of the night to bring his presents. We got bikes every year; I think my mother, Vergie, supplied us with some of those bikes one year because she was living up north as well. All the kids loved to skate; we were the first ones to have roller derby skates.

I remember the year before when Annie Mae got her skates. She had the old kind where you had to put the skates together and lock them with a key.

Pete, Lisa, and I, along with Annie Mae, had a bunch of gifts. Annie Mae was older than we were, so she got the "old people" toys. One year for Christmas, Annie Mae got a doll that was damn near four feet tall. That doll was ugly as hell. My grandmother would always say, "Did you all open up my gifts that I got for y'all?"

We kind of knew what her gifts were; it was either a pair of socks, a hat, neckties, peppermint candy, gloves, or some of those orange slice candies. Every now and then, my grandmother would give us some undergarments. As I think about it now, my grandmother didn't have to buy us anything because our aunts and uncles bought mostly everything. Sometimes my brother and I would get Christmas cards with money in them. We had money and toys—we were rich! You couldn't tell us anything. We had the best of the best.

My cousin Evelyn always came over and said her dream was to see a 'White Christmas.' One year, she got her wish because when we were awakened for Christmas, snow was on the ground. I wished I could get those Carver Courts Christmas days back; when we moved out of Carver Courts, Christmas was never the same.

CHAPTER 10

Meeting My Father for the First Time

One evening, while playing in the yard in Carver Courts, a strange man came over to my grandmother's place, looking at me kind of strange, and I didn't know who he was. I think either my Aunt Denderant or my Aunt Mavis was home at the time; they were sitting on the porch. I looked at them, and they said, "That is your father."

I think maybe my father was coming back from Vietnam, finally paying us a visit. I think I was six or seven years old; I really don't know. I think this man brought a bike to the house. It was strange when they said, "This is your father," because to me, my father was already dead.

My grandfather died on May 19, 1970, and he was the only father I ever knew; as a matter of fact, we called my grandfather "Daddy." Anyway, this guy with a mustache came over to speak to me, and I really didn't know what to say. He knew me, but I didn't know him. I think I asked him his name; I can't recall what he said.

Anyway, his name was Milton Dove Jr., but as the future predicted, he has never been called by this name. The only person that called him Milton Dove was my grandfather who was alive, and my grandfather's name is Milton Dove Sr. My father and grandfather have an auto shop together called Dove and Son's Garage.

My grandfather would often call him Milton Jr., but everyone in Kinston would call him his famous nickname, "Meat Dove." How and why he got this name, I will never know.

Getting back to how we met, everything was silent with my aunts; you couldn't hear a word. They were staring at my reaction, and my reaction was just like any kid who meets a stranger. I felt very uncomfortable. I can't recall our conversation, but I'm quite sure it was short because I didn't know what to say. Maybe my aunts were quiet because I really looked like the guy, and maybe it was confirmed that I was his child by our looks.

My Father, 'Meat Dove' When He Was Younger

*A Photo of Me, When I Was Near His
Age in the Above Photo*

It was rumored that my father denied my brother as his child. If that was the case, my aunts were probably saying to themselves, "There's no way he can deny him."

Shortly after talking with my father, he went on about his business.

I remember my father coming to my grandmother's apartment again. He asked my grandmother if he could take me for a ride; I can't recall what kind of car he had, but I know it was green. He took me to McDonald's and bought me a cheeseburger and some fries. For some strange reason, he asked me how my asthma was doing. I couldn't figure out how he knew about my asthma; I'm sure my mother, Vergie, told him this because she usually tells him everything. I found this out later—that my mother told my father everything about his kids.

While I was eating and talking with my father, all of a sudden, he asked me a strange question. He asked me if I was afraid of dying because of my asthma. I don't remember what I said, but I did find out that he had asthma. My Aunt Denderant used to say something similar to this.

Whenever I would have an asthma attack, she would say with her fast-talking self, "Boy, are you going to die????? Because you need to let somebody know."

Man, my Aunt Denderant would say some wild shit. After I finished eating, my father took me back home. He wouldn't come around that much, but I do remember when he came around and picked me up on his motorcycle.

He took me riding down Queen Street, going about one hundred miles per hour! That was the last time I would ever ride on his motorcycle. I realized this man was crazy!

When I found out where my father's shop was, I would often go over there and ask him for some money. As a matter of fact, I could see my father's shop from Carver Courts. I found out very fast how stingy my father was.

"The only way you can get some money from me is you work for it," he made this very clear.

When I asked my father for fifty cents, he would tell me to go get the broom and sweep the garage. Not only did he mean that, he would always ask me a thousand questions: "What do you need the money for? When do you need it?"

I didn't care about how many questions he asked; the only thing I cared about was getting that fifty cents. My brother would do the same thing; he would go over to the shop and ask my father for some money, and he'd get asked a thousand questions as well. My brother didn't have the patience that I had; he wasn't going to beg you for a damn thing.

Anyway, when Pete did ask my father for some money, my father told him to go get in his truck. Naturally, my brother did as he was told. My father drove him to the Kinston Daily Free

Press and immediately got him a job as a paperboy. I don't know how long my brother kept the job, but he didn't ask my father for any more money, and he didn't go back to the shop.

I was the one who kept going back to the shop asking for money. When I was about eleven years old, my father would come by my grandmother's apartment and take us to get some school clothes.

Even though my father was stingy as hell, he would take us to the most expensive stores in Kinston—like H. Stadium and Brody's. They had good quality clothes, but I would later find out why my father took us to these expensive clothing stores. He took us to these places because when you bought clothes from them, you didn't have to worry about those clothes wearing out as easily because of the material they were made from; it wasn't cheap. This meant my father didn't have to buy us clothes as often.

Still, when I was around my father, the conversation was short because I didn't know what to say. When my brother and I would go to his family reunion, his family would stare at us, especially his sisters. This was uncomfortable because I only knew my father's youngest sister, Lorna. She and I were only a year apart. I didn't know my father's oldest sisters, Velma, Timber, and Kaye. I hadn't been around my father's family that much.

I would hear his sisters saying, "He looks just like Bunky." My father's sister called him by another one of his nicknames.

My brother and I would get in a corner to ourselves and wouldn't say anything. It seemed like everyone knew each other, but we didn't know them. The only people my brother and I knew were the workers at my father's shop, and we spoke with them. My brother and I were ready to go home.

As I said earlier, my father was stingy, and whenever he could find a way to save some money, he would. My father built us a go-kart and came to my grandmother's house; we had recently moved out of the projects. He asked my grandmother if he could take us riding on the go-kart.

It was a Saturday afternoon. He took us to the Kinston Shirt Factory parking lot; the people who worked there didn't work on Saturdays, and their parking lot was big but empty. When we got out of my father's truck, he asked who wanted to ride first, and of course, I said I did. He showed me where the gas and brake pedals were. He cranked up the go-kart, and I drove that thing like I was at a NASCAR racing competition.

My brother didn't want to ride the go-kart, but my father made him ride it anyway. While my brother was riding the go-kart, either the brakes went out or he panicked because he ran the go-kart up under another car and messed up his legs. My brother hated my father for that, and to this day, he still resents him.

When we went back home, my grandmother was furious. She didn't much care for my father, but she never said that around us. You could see it in her eyes. My brother's relationship with my father grew further apart, and today, they still don't have a relationship. This wasn't because of the go-kart incident; it was because my brother never cared for our father.

I think it was because my brother may have found out the rumor that my father denied him was true. It is enough to be denied, but to hold a grudge for this long is something else. I'm the one that is notorious for holding grudges, not my brother. I never asked my father if he denied my brother, and I never asked my brother why he doesn't like our father. To tell you the truth, I really can't say my brother is holding a grudge against my father; he just doesn't associate himself with him. He was my biological father, but my grandfather, Mr. Wesley Jones, was my father until the day he died; my Uncle Jay and Hamm took up the slack and were like dads for us before they had their own children.

CHAPTER 11

The KKK

When I was growing up, I used to be a batboy for the baseball team my Uncle Jay played for. I think the name of the team was "Dapp's Party Store." When they would go to Smithfield, North Carolina—in my opinion, known as KKK country—most of the team would have to put guns in the trunk of the car because the people in Smithfield were known to start shit with Black people.

When the team arrived in Smithfield to play ball, we could see the rednecks ready to start trouble as soon as we hit the field. The umpire, who was from Smithfield, would make as many bad calls against our team as he could. You had to be perfect just to beat the team from Smithfield. You could hear the fans in the stands saying, "You niggers better leave before it turns dark!" Little did they know, once they started trouble, the guys on our team had something for them! It was going to be an all-out war once the fans and the other team started trouble. Blacks were tired of dealing with the KKK from Smithfield, N.C.

When you drove through the town, you would always get stopped and given a ticket, and you better not say a bad word to the officer, or you were going down to the station and getting your ass whipped. In today's time, law enforcement will whip your ass wherever they stop you; most times, you don't make it to the station, and in some extreme cases, you end up dead.

I don't know how the atmosphere is in Smithfield today, but I do know that when I drive through there, I'm very careful not to break any rules...the Klan still exists. In 1992, the Klan marched through downtown Kinston heading to Grifton, North Carolina. I was surprised, but in the First Amendment, there is a clause that says, "You have the freedom to assemble," but the policemen were nervous about the situation. I even saw the Kinston S.W.A.T. team on top of buildings because they felt there was going to be a fight, but to my surprise, it went alright.

I really didn't start to learn about racism until I started school; I guess my grandmother never took time out to tell us about it, maybe because she didn't want to pollute our minds. The older folks knew about it, but I guess the younger children didn't know about it. We were too busy playing in the neighborhood. The only thing I knew was that Blacks stayed in one section of town and whites stayed in another section.

When I was going to Lewis Elementary School, my music teacher was a white lady named Mrs. Simms. She slapped me in the face with her hands for talking—she will always regret doing that.

My mother was staying in D.C. at the time, and I think she had just come home to visit for a couple of days. I think my Uncle Jay was either a guidance counselor or he taught the sixth grade. I came home and told my mother what had happened. The next day she went to school with me and was ready to jump on the teacher. I think the principal of the school had to call Jay from his office to cool things off. Of course, Jay knew how his sister was—wild and crazy. The only thing I know is that Mrs. Simms never put her hands on me again. I wasn't the only student Mrs. Simms slapped. She slapped another student in the face, and his nose started to bleed. The student's name was Adam Foster; he was a year older than I was. How this lady got away with this shit, I don't know. Adam's mother came to the school and informed the teacher she didn't have any problems with her disciplining her child if he acted up, but she better not ever put her hands in his face again, and as the mother was talking, the teacher slammed the door in her face. Adam's mother took the hinges off the door and went in and choked the teacher; two teachers broke up the fight. The teacher resigned the next week.

As I've grown older, I can look back and see there was racism at the swimming pool. The Blacks would go swim at Holloway or Lovett Hines Pool, and the whites would go swim at Emma Webb Pool. If Blacks went to Emma Webb Pool, the staff didn't make you get out of the pool, but somehow, you knew you didn't belong there.

When I got older, my family ended up leaving the projects and moving right around the corner from Emma Webb Pool. There were several movie theaters we attended. Most of the Blacks attended the State Theater on South Queen Street; I would pay fifty cents to get in the movie. I never saw a white person at that theater; I only saw whites at the Paramount and the Park Theater. Both places charged seventy-five cents to get in. When we didn't have the money, we would sneak into the movies. I can even recall my friend Antray and I trying to sneak into the movies.

There was an alley located in the back of the Paramount Theater; it was easy to open the back door of the theater. One Sunday, when we didn't have any money, we went in the back of the Paramount Theater and opened the door while the movie was playing; we crawled on our knees through the curtains until we found a seat and mixed in with the crowd. What we didn't know was that in the balcony, one of the staff members saw us come through the door.

While we were in our seats, two staff members came, a man named Clyde and a lady named Bonnie. Clyde pointed us out, and Antray took off running; before I could take off running, the staff grabbed me.

"Bonnie, call the police!!!!!!!!!!!!!!!!!!!!!!!!" Clyde said when we got up to the front office.

My heart started beating real fast because I knew what was going to happen when I got home.

"You must have me mixed up with someone else," I told Clyde.

"No, I didn't! I saw you and your friend sneaking in through the back door!"

I looked down below my feet and saw a lot of ticket stubs on the floor. I bent down as if I were tying my shoe and slipped one of the ticket stubs in my pocket. When the police came, Clyde told them I had broken in through the back door of the movie with one of my friends, but the other friend ran off.

"I didn't know the man that ran. I didn't sneak into the movies. I have my ticket stub here in my pocket," I said to the police.

Bonnie looked at my ticket stub and compared it with the tickets they had sold that day and said, "He can't be the one because his ticket stub matches what we sold today."

All of a sudden, I got brave… "I told you all that you had the wrong person."

Bonnie said, "Clyde, let him go back into the movies."

The police left, and I went back inside the theater. My heart was beating so hard that I couldn't enjoy the movie, thinking that they might come out and get me again; the name of the movie that was playing was called "The Greatest," featuring Muhammad Ali. I felt like I had just gotten out of the greatest trouble that I had ever been in.

CHAPTER 12

I Was a Devious Kid

When I was growing up in Carver Courts, I did some devious things that I consider devious. My friends and I used to go around and ring people's doorbells—and before they could open the door, we would take off running. Doing these types of devious things was funny. It was so funny that we added more fun to it. We would set bottles at people's doors, ring the doorbell, and take off running; when they opened the door, the bottles would break. We would be somewhere in the bushes, laughing our asses off. If my grandmother ever found out that I'd done these things growing up, she would be mad because she taught me how to behave myself.

My friends and I stole little petty things from the stores, things like moon pies, oatmeal cakes, and potato chips. I remember going to Mr. Frank's store; we knew he couldn't half see, and we'd steal things right in front of his face. None of the kids needed to steal anything because we all came from good backgrounds. Our families supplied us with what we needed. It's ironic that the people who don't need anything are the main ones who go out and get into trouble for the hell of it. This is not cool!

I'm ashamed of my past, and if you are reading this book and you have done the same things that I've done, you should be ashamed too!

My stealing days ended quickly, or at least I thought they did. I think kids do things because of peer pressure and the challenge of, "Let me do this to see whether or not I can get away with it." The last time I ever stole anything was at a store called "Gibbs." We had always heard that Mr. Gibbs was a Klansman, but whether or not that was true is another story; I'm not going to try to validate something I don't know. Me and one of my friends, named Lonnie, went to Gibbs Supermarket to steal things for the party we used to have with the kids in the neighborhood. Lonnie was the ringleader; we would pitch in ten or fifteen cents to purchase cookies, hotdogs, hotdog rolls, chili, ketchup, mustard, and chips. Me and Lonnie would steal most of the items and go to the counter to pay for the rest of the items.

That was a bold move on our part; we were paying for the items while having stolen items in the waist of our pants.

On this one occasion, we went into Mr. Gibbs' store; I think I stole a can of meat or something. I can't remember what it was, but I remember Lonnie and I were right beside each other; Lonnie was smooth when he was stealing. He would steal, and both of us would cover by looking to see if anyone was watching.

He said, "Hey man, there goes Mr. Gibbs; go ahead on and put that out of your pants and put it back!"

Lonnie put his things back real smooth and walked away; I was trying to put my item back, but somehow, the canned food got stuck between my belt. I was trying so, so hard to get that canned food out of my belt, and Gibbs caught me...

"I ought to call the police," he said. "Julie, call the police!"

Julie said, "Naw, I'm not going to call the police. I know his mother, and I'll pay for it myself. Then I'll tell his mother on him."

Julie knew that my mother didn't stay in North Carolina anymore, but she knew I stayed with my grandmother. Julie was a small, nice white lady who really helped people out. She got along with Blacks. Her husband was a police officer, and she and my mother were very close.

Mrs. Julie called the house, but my grandmother wasn't there, so my Uncle Hamm came and picked me up and took me home. When my grandmother found out what I had done, she beat the hell out of me, and my stealing days were over. To this day, I have never stolen anything again.

I remember when my brother Pete and my cousin Eric got caught stealing. This incident took place on a Saturday. I came in the house with my basketball, and my grandmother was ironing clothes in the pantry; my Aunt Denderant was in the kitchen.

Denderant said, "What were you doing out there stealing?" I didn't have a clue what she was talking about.

"How did you get away from the police station so fast? Jay just left to go down to the police station to pick you up. I don't know why the police let you go when we told them we were sending someone down there to pick you up."

Denderant hit me side the head.

"I wasn't stealing; I just came off the basketball court!"

"You are lying!"

I couldn't convince her that I wasn't stealing. My grandmother rolled her eyes and said, "Garry, what did you steal?"

"No ma'am, I didn't steal anything."

After my grandmother asked me about stealing, Jay walked in the house with Pete. Pete was the one who was stealing. Denderant and my grandmother couldn't believe it. Pete was a laid-back "A and B" student who never got into trouble and never caused any headaches for my family. When the police called the house and said, "We have your grandson down at the station for stealing; could you please come and pick him up?" immediately, my family thought it was me. They appeared to be disappointed that it was Pete and not me.

Jay's feelings were hurt because Pete had asked Jay if he would give him some money to go downtown to buy him something. Pete had the money, but he didn't pay for the items. He and my cousin Eric were on a roll.

Eric managed not to get caught, but Pete told them that Eric was stealing too. My grandmother called her nephew Johnny Lee; this was Eric's father, and told him that Eric was downtown stealing with Pete.

Earlier in the book, I said my grandmother would step in and stop my aunts and uncles from disciplining us if it was petty, but she didn't stop Jay this time.

Jay took Pete upstairs and started beating the hell out of him with his belt. Jay was beating Pete so hard that I started crying. I left the house and walked a few steps away. I heard Johnny Lee beating the hell out of Eric, and Eric was screaming just as loud as Pete. We stayed in the 8th building, and Eric and his parents stayed in the 9th building. I walked into the cemetery that was across the street from Carver Courts and started thinking about what had gone on between Eric and Pete. I was very surprised by Pete stealing. Neither Pete nor Eric was able to go out of the house for about a week.

If parents were to start back disciplining their kids the way we were disciplined, a lot of kids would not be in as much trouble as they are today. Today parents are afraid of their kids; they are afraid of what social services would do to them. The only thing the kids have to say when their parents are being disciplined is, "They are going to call social services," and the discipline stops. We have allowed the government to frighten us when it comes to disciplining our children. Yet, the government wants to know why these Black kids are the way they are—out of control.

I understand that some parents go overboard when they discipline their kids, and social services have to step in. I'm not making light of kids being abused, but some of the things are not child abuse. If that was the case, all of our parents in the past should be locked up because they whipped some ass back in the day.

I notice that most of the kids who weren't disciplined when they got into trouble are either dead, in prison, or on drugs. The shame of it all is that we have become so societal-wise, meaning that we allow the government to step in when, in the old days, if a child got his behind beat, he would never think about calling the police.

We didn't think of calling the police and were afraid of the repercussions that would occur if we dialed 911; you had to move or go stay with the policeman that came to the house when you called. It is not the same today. The school teacher is afraid to spank the children; when we were spanked at school, someone told our parents, and you got a whipping from your parents that same day.

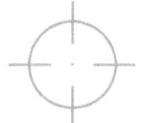

CHAPTER 13

Legal Hustler

Growing up as a kid, I was what you would call a "legal hustler." I made money any way I could, but it was always legal. It all started in elementary school. The schools would have "candy selling drives" for different charities or something the school needed. If the students wanted to participate, they could volunteer to take a case of candy bars home and sell them.

At the end of the candy drive, the students could win prizes for selling the most candy or cookies or whatever the school was selling. You had 1st place, 2nd place, and 3rd place; of course, I wanted 1st place.

I would take a case of candy home and go door to door asking people if they wanted to buy some candy. The candy bar was small, but the school would charge a dollar for each candy bar. Most of the people who bought the candy knew they could go to the store and buy four candy bars for what we were charging, but it was for a good cause, which is why the people bought them.

I didn't let the "hard customers" get away easy. I had my own game and charm for them. I would just smile and say, "I want to win a prize, sir or madam. Could you just buy the candy so I can win?" Sometimes, after I got through talking, the customer would buy three bars instead of just one—they couldn't resist what I found out later was called "charm." My grandmother, Tessie Jones, didn't get off easy either. She would take about ten bars to work and sell them; within a day or two, a case of candy was sold. I would go back to school and ask for two more cases, and then it turned into three cases—I was on a roll. The teachers wouldn't say who was in the lead, but I knew I had to be in the top three because I wasn't going to let anyone win over me in getting that 1st place prize.

After the contest was over, the school would hold some kind of awards day and announce who sold the most candy, and when they said "Garry Jones," I walked my cool ass up there on stage and accepted that cheap prize they had in store for me. I can't remember what the prize was, but I know it was cheap. I had sold about $100 worth of candy and probably only got a $5 prize.

I would go home and tell my grandmother that I had won; she was more excited than I was. My grandmother knew I was a special kid, but she didn't know how special I was. I not only sold candy in the hood, but my buddy Vince, a.k.a. Bunny, and I would borrow his father's lawn mower and cut grass to make plenty of money.

I would knock on the door and ask, "Do you want me to cut your grass for you?"

"Yes," some would say.

I turned to Bunny and said, "Let's do it!"

My job was to police the yards and pick up any rocks, big branches, cans, and anything that would mess up the blade of the lawn mower. When I was finished, Bunny would cut the person's yard as if it was someone getting a haircut at a barber shop. That's how good Bunny could cut a yard.

Bunny's father would ask for a cut of the money because we were using his lawn mower, but we fixed that real quick; we gave him his cut but kept cutting every week or every two weeks and saved the money. Eventually, we had enough saved up to buy us a new lawn mower, and his father couldn't get any of our money.

When Bunny and I weren't cutting grass, we would pop popcorn and make lemonade and take it out on the basketball court, then we'd sell it to the guys who were playing ball, even though both of us were athletes as well. We made our money first, then we played ball afterward.

The other guys in the hood had their hustle, but they couldn't take our customers; their customers were loyal to us. I had my own hustle on the side without Bunny.

People in the hood, as well as most other people, drank those Pepsis and Dr. Peppers, especially the older folks; they would put peanuts in their sodas. I would have me a grocery cart and go to every door asking for people's bottles. I would then sell the bottles to a man named Mr. Campbell. He would give me three cents for every bottle, and then he would take the bottles to the plant and they would give him five cents for every bottle.

When I wasn't selling bottles, I would be selling Kings Chapel Tea—that's the church that my grandmother was a member of. They had their own tea bags in their boxes with their church name on them. It was only right that I sold the tea because my grandmother hustled for me, and so I hustled to help her out. Nickel and diming wasn't good enough for me, so I had to step my hustle game up...

My Aunt Colleen (Mavis) would read the Jet magazines and cut out things that the magazines were advertising for you to sell. This particular advertisement that was popular was getting people's social security numbers and asking them if they wanted their social security cards made out of metal with the government symbol on them. I would take the orders for $2, and my aunt would mail the company $1 for each order taken while I kept a dollar.

Metal Social Security Cards I Used To Sell

I became rich doing that because, hell, you had to sell a lot of bottles to make a dollar, and I made a dollar with one order. Of course, my aunt wouldn't let me spend all of my money at one time, so she would take some of the money and save it for me. I remember my cousin Annie Mae was in high school and they had the Miss Cotillion Contest—Black folks call it the Miss Cotillion

Ball, but white folks call it the Debutante Ball; guess who they called on to help Ann compete and win third place? They called 'The Hustler.'

My grandmother was the best cook in the world, and even though I don't like sweet potato pies, my grandmother would make the pies and I, "The Hustler," would go out and sell them like hotcakes. Ann probably would have gotten 1st place if my grandmother had made her banana pudding and told me to go out and sell it.

The 1st, 2nd, and 3rd places weren't too different. I wished she would have gotten 1st place because I worked my butt off. Third place was not good enough for me, but the fact is, if more money was donated and if we didn't have to sell pies, Ann could have taken the grand prize home.

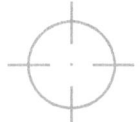

CHAPTER 14

Falling Out in the Cucumber Field

Growing up in the projects, Mr. Earl, one of my friend's fathers, had his own truck and would recruit guys from the neighborhood who wanted to work in the tobacco and cucumber fields in the country. I always wanted to go, but I had asthma, and asking my grandmother if I could go was downright crazy... I knew the answer.

The fellows who went got paid on Fridays. They would work from sunup to sundown, and on Fridays they would flash the money they made. Of course, my little $5 a week couldn't compare to the $100 they made.

Earl's son Vince, a.k.a. Bunny, would always take me downtown with him when he spent his money. He would buy his school clothes and treat me to hot dogs and sodas at a store called 'Roses.' Bunny would also give me five dollars to spend, which made me feel like I had ten dollars.

My mind couldn't stand seeing them with all that money while I couldn't get in on the action. One morning around 6:00 a.m., I decided to get up and sneak out of the window to catch the cucumber truck; of course, the people who worked in the cucumber field didn't make as much as those in the tobacco field.

Little did I know that you couldn't work all day in one hundred-degree weather without having eaten breakfast and without plenty to drink. When I got to the cucumber field, eating cucumbers became my breakfast until I began to feel sick and really dizzy. Nicole and Earl's daughter, Jennifer, went to tell the white man what was happening to me. The white man called the ambulance and told me not to come back.

On the way to the hospital, I think Jennifer and Nicole rode in the ambulance with me. While riding in the ambulance, I could feel myself getting better because of the air conditioning. When I got to the hospital, someone had to call my grandmother; I don't know who called, but my mind was racing with the thought of what she was going to do or say.

When you go to the hospital, they don't let you go right away. You have to stay there while they run tests before you are released. I think my uncle Jay came to pick me up. When I got home, my grandmother looked at me, rolled her eyes, and told me, "Sit at the kitchen table and eat your supper (dinner)."

She had cooked fried chicken and some pork n' beans; that was the best chicken and pork n' beans I had ever had in my life.

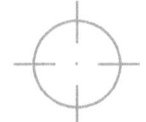

CHAPTER 15

Carver Courts Socials

Carver Courts Center is where the socials were held. The center was a recreational facility where kids could come in and play ping pong, cards, and shoot pool, and on the weekends at night, the 'socials' were held. Carver Courts socials were the bomb, and everybody from across town used to come over to our social.

When I was a kid, I was told not to go to the socials because I was too young and a fight might break out. In actuality, it was very rare to find a fight at the social. Everyone was trying to outdance one another.

I remember when the staff at the Carver Courts Center first painted the 'Soul Train' line. The Soul Train line was red, black, and green, and the Soul Train picture looked just like the one from the show 'Soul Train' back in the 70s. The socials were held mostly on Friday and Saturday nights. You had to pay a quarter to get in, but I would sneak in; if I didn't sneak in, there was always someone at the door who knew me. I knew I was too young to be in there because you had to be sixteen, but they didn't say anything.

The staff member in charge of opening up the center was Roland Tate. Roland would give instructions not to let anyone in if they weren't sixteen, and then he would leave and come back in time to lock up the place.

When it was time to dance on the soul train line, it was just like on TV. The girls would line up on one side, and the guys would line up on the other, each going down the soul train line jamming. Of course, I was young and couldn't dance; as a matter of fact, I can't dance now, but I went down the line anyway with my moves.

The socials would end around midnight. They ran mostly everybody out, and then the staff would clean up. The crowd would go hang on the block, and that's when the fights broke out. A lot of people used to look out for me, especially King George; he made sure no one touched me until I got home.

I remember when George and Jack Williams had shootouts. George was representing Carver Courts (The Block), and Jack Williams was representing Mitchell Wooten Courts (The Front). These two guys didn't like each other, and when they saw each other, they would take their guns out and stand behind cars and shoot at one another. Needless to say, neither one of them got shot. It reminded you of the 'Wild, Wild West'; they had their fights as well.

I really don't think they were trying to hit each other when they were shooting; they were sending a message: you stay on your side of town, and I will stay on mine.

The legends in Carver Courts were people like King George, my Uncle John (Jay Jay) Jones, my Uncle Earl (Hamm- Mr. Biggs) Jones, Hook Jones, Johnny Tuff, James Freeman, Nellie Q, Zeek Raspberry, Pop Hussey, Shack Hart, Kemoe Dixon, Tyrone Warren, Don Pitman, Dooley Wilkes, James Bay-boy Irvin, Skull, Wink Eye, Jim Danny, Lee Lee, and a lot of other good brothers.

George was the best at getting you what you needed. He would take your order for anything you wanted and come back the same day with what you ordered. George is the only person who stole shit and never got caught.

Someone wanted a T.V., and George went to some appliance place. While he was in there, he went to the front counter and asked someone, "Can you open the door so I can take my T.V. out?" The workers didn't know they were opening the door for George to steal their merchandise.

George was the Robin Hood of Carver Courts. He and his boys, Thomas, Carter, Chris (Doc), and Lendel, would break into a grocery store, steal all the groceries, come back to Carver Courts, fire up the grill, and feed anyone who wanted to eat for free. We were eating steaks, pork chops, chicken, whatever you named; George and his crew had it. They were drinking wine, beer, sodas, and smoking cigarettes.

George never got caught in action, but he always went to prison because someone snitched on him, though he refused to snitch on anyone else. If anyone came over to Carver Courts and didn't stay there and started trouble, George would take out his sawed-off shotgun and go looking for those people. He also fought with his hands. I must admit these guys today are law-abiding citizens.

CHAPTER 16

There Was Something Different About Me

I was a different kid, not because I suffered from depression, asthma, and ulcers, and not because I was made to go to church, Vacation Bible School, and Sunday School, but because I wasn't satisfied when I didn't get answers to the questions I asked people.

My school teachers would always say, "You ask too many questions." There were other adults who weren't teachers that would say, "Man, you ask too many damn questions." Little did I know that I had another side to me, a spiritual one. I can't say that side came from church, even though I had to go; I would cut up in church and couldn't tell you what the sermons were about. When I was small, I would often find a spot somewhere by myself and sing to God... I don't mean singing words to God because I couldn't sing, but I would sing God a hymn.

To this day, I haven't forgotten how the tune went. I have always known that God would be a part of my life, but I never knew in what way. He didn't keep me on this earth for nothing. I don't know why God is allowing me to still live in this world because if it were up to me, I would have clocked out a long time ago; but committing suicide is not the way to get to heaven. I often pray and ask God what my purpose is in this world. I'm still praying for the answer to that question, but I don't have one yet. Maybe if I stopped breaking those 'Ten Commandments' and aligned myself with His will, I might finally hear from Him.

There's an old saying: dying is easy, but living is hard—especially when you're trying to do the right thing. Every time I thought I was getting myself together, something in this world would pull my focus away. I found out later in life that this is how satan works. When you try to live God's way, satan fights hard to pull you away from Him. You notice I spelled satan without a capital; I refuse to give him any credit. His name doesn't deserve to be spelled correctly.

When I was a child, I would always go to the cemetery and talk to God, but He never answered me back. Some people say they can hear God's voice, and they say His voice sounds like water coming out of an ocean. I need to hear that before I can believe it. I've heard that God speaks through the Holy Spirit when He wants to talk with you, but whatever the case may be, He still hasn't told me what I'm here for. Until He does, I guess I'll keep listening for Him. I should have been dead a long time ago, and later in this book, you will see what I'm talking about.

CHAPTER 17

Leaving Carver Courts

300 Summit Avenue

Moving out of Carver Courts was one of the hardest things to deal with in my life; the thought of leaving my friends was terrifying.

It was January 14, 1977, on a Saturday evening when we actually moved. I had lived in Carver Courts for twelve years, eleven months, and two weeks. I was mad as hell. I didn't want to live in a house! I wanted to live in the projects!

This was a devastating blow for me; I didn't know how to handle not waking up, going to the basketball court, and playing in the Carver Courts Center. My family tried to make up for it by putting a basketball court in our backyard.

The only good thing about waking up on January 15, 1977, was looking forward to seeing the Super Bowl. The Oakland Raiders and the Minnesota Vikings were playing. The Cowboys weren't playing—they were, and still are, my team. The Cowboys had just lost the year before to the Pittsburgh Steelers when Jackie Smith dropped that touchdown pass in the end zone.

I wanted to be back in Carver Courts so badly that I literally rode my bike back in the morning just to walk to school with my friends. I didn't give a damn about catching the bus. After school, I walked back to Carver Courts as if I still lived there. I played with my friends and rode my bike back to my new home.

Denderant, my grandmother, and the rest of the family were elated; their dreams were to leave the projects, but my dreams were to stay in the projects until death. I was still a kid; I didn't know any better. What my family was doing was trying to own something instead of paying rent all the time. I always said once I got older I would go back and live in Carver Courts, but that never happened.

My Grandmother in her front yard.

A kid couldn't understand this concept until they got older. The longer we stayed in the new house, the more I was able to adjust to my new environment. It took me about three years to adjust. Whenever the New Year would come around, I would try my best to bring in the New Year at Carver Courts. It was hard to forget where I came from. When the clock struck midnight, I would holler, "Happy New Year!" Then I would walk back to my house, which was fifteen minutes away.

I didn't realize how blessed I was; the brick home was nice and beautiful, and we had our own fireplace. I was too blind to see what God blessed our family with because I was blinded by Carver Courts.

Pete and I still had to share a bedroom. My grandmother had the master bedroom, Denderant had the next largest room, and Pete and I had the smallest room. Ann had gone to college, and Mavis had moved to Raleigh, North Carolina. Jay had already moved out, but he was still considered the man of the house because we were still punished whenever we got in trouble or our grades dropped.

I really didn't appreciate what I had because I didn't like real food unless it was fried chicken, pork chops, and mashed potatoes. I loved junk food, and that's why I stayed sick all the time. The doctor used to tell my grandmother that I needed to take vitamins.

On Friday evenings, I knew what the menu was: fish that still had the eyeball in it, cornbread, and maybe cabbage. My grandmother used to give me money every Friday because she knew I wasn't going to eat what she cooked. I took those couple of dollars and went to McDonald's.

I must admit, my grandmother spoiled me.

It was hard for my grandmother to stop cooking those big meals after we moved into our house. I guess when you've been cooking for a big family for a long time, you continue to prepare big meals. My grandmother was happy to move. I could see it all over her body; she had that swagger when she got around her friends and was proud to go to work. She would wake me up and give me lunch money and a couple more pennies so I could get a cinnamon roll or a milkshake for lunch.

She made sure her grandchildren had everything, even if she had to go without it herself. When I went on my sporting trips or just school trips in general, she would ensure that I had money. She would soon get her money back during the summer when I got a job.

CHAPTER 18

The Trainer

In the fall of 1977, I was a trainer for the Kinston High Football Team. I was under the supervision of a teacher named Mr. Johnny Shepherd. Mr. Shepherd gave me, Tony Hill, and Eric Koonce the trainer's job. He taught us how to wrap ankles and attend to minor injuries for the varsity football team. Mr. Shepherd made us feel like we could do anything.

Not everyone made the traveling squad, even some of the players, but Mr. Shepherd carried his trainers everywhere he went. I was his main man. The only thing I hated about my position was giving water to the team during game night.

Whenever there was a timeout on the football field, somehow Eric would dodge this job; he would be somewhere else. Eric has always been slick ever since we were kids; he and I were second cousins. The players would ask you to bring the water out on the field, and when you ran with the water, they would tell you to go back. Before you could go back to the sidelines, they'd tell you to bring the water back again. I used to be mad as hell because they had a big five-gallon container of water with about five nozzles on it and a pump in the middle.

In order for the water to come out of the nozzles, you had to keep pumping the pump until the water came up to the nozzles. I used to have to run with that container until the water came out during the timeout. When the players were winning, I would bring the water on the field, and they'd be happy and start joking during timeouts, but when they were losing, they'd tell me, "Get that damn water out of here!"

I used to be pissed at those players. So, after the season, I said I wasn't going to be a trainer anymore. It was good while it lasted, but I wasn't going to take that abuse.

After the season, I went to work for my father. At first, I started working only on Saturdays, cleaning up the garage for two hours and getting paid $75 a month. Considering I wasn't a trainer anymore, my father asked me to work after school from 4 p.m. to 6 p.m. I agreed.

When I got out of school, I would go back to Carver Courts where my cousin lived and change clothes, and then I would walk across the cemetery to the shop. My responsibilities were to clean the bathroom, sweep the floor, and clean the tools. It was still quiet between my father and me because we didn't have that much to say. He might quiz me on some math to see what I knew. I would answer his questions and continue to clean up.

I tried out for my eighth-grade basketball team, but Coach Little cut me during the final cut. I was crushed. I actually went home and cried my heart out. My father asked me if I wanted to work full-time instead of just Saturdays. I really didn't want to, but I loved money and said, "Yes."

I would leave school (weekdays) and go to work. To tell you the truth, all of my work was done in the first forty-five minutes, and I really didn't have anything to do until 5:45 p.m. When the shop began to close, that's when all the sweeping was done. My father and I still didn't have much of a conversation. I would look at him as he strolled around, cool with that cigarette in his mouth.

There was a song that came on the radio called "Everyone Plays the Fool." I forgot which group sang it, but whenever my father would hear that song, he would get his 'pimp walk' on. My paternal grandfather would just stare at me all the time; he never would say anything. When customers would come to the shop and see me, they'd say, "Meat, that's got to be your goddamn son; he looks just like you! Meat, you can't deny him! That little motherfucker looks just like you."

"Young man, what's your mother's name?" This is what they would ask.

I remember walking down Queen Street when a man looked at me and said, "Son, I don't know who you are, but you've got to be Meat Dove's son."

"Yes, I am," is all I would say.

My father had a temper back then, but he was also a hustler—not in a sense that would cause him to go to jail, but he knew how to make money.

I remember him saying, "Goldwater, go over to that house across from the cemetery and clean it up."

He gave me the key, and I didn't ask any questions. When I got over there, I would see beer bottles, cigarettes, and playing cards. I cleaned it up and still didn't ask any questions. Every week, I would go over and clean up. Often, when I cleaned, I would find change lying on the floor. One day it hit me: this is a gambling house! But of course, I never told my father I knew what the house was; it was obvious.

On one particular day, my father found out that the school was having a teacher's workday (which meant I didn't have to go to school). The next day, he called me and said, "I want you to come to work from 8 a.m. to 6 p.m."

I didn't like this shit because whenever we didn't have to go to school, I wanted to stay and hang out with my friends. I told him I would be in. When I reported to work, I didn't have a smile on my face.

"What's wrong with you?"

"Nothing," I said, going to grab the broom and sweep a little bit.

Right before he took his lunch break, my father said, "Goldwater (my nickname), I want you to go upstairs and get the swing blade and cut down the weeds over by the old junk cars."

When he came back from lunch, I could smell alcohol on his breath.

"Goldwater, I thought I told you to get that damn swing blade and cut those damn weeds down."

Mr. Dove (my grandfather) didn't pay me to do that; he only paid me to clean the tools, sweep the floor, and clean the bathroom.

"What did you say?"

I repeated it back to him.

"If you don't take your motherfucking ass upstairs and get that goddamn swing blade and cut down those weeds, I will beat your motherfucking ass!"

I dropped the rag I had in my hands and walked away.

"Bring your goddamn ass back here!"

I kept walking, and then I could hear his footsteps, so I took off running. When I turned around, I saw him take his cap off and start chasing me through the cemetery, but he couldn't catch me. As a matter of fact, one time, he was gaining ground on me because I was scared, and my legs felt numb, but he still wasn't able to catch me. I knew he was headed straight to my cousin's apartment in Carver Courts because he knew I changed clothes over there. But I outsmarted him and ran into Mrs. Sue's apartment.

My father ran to my cousin's house like I expected him to do. When he got there, my cousin told him, "You need to leave before I call my father because Goldwater isn't here." I told Mrs. Sue to call my house and tell my grandmother that my father was trying to jump on me. My grandmother sent my Uncle Hamm to come pick me up.

I was petrified even though I knew I was safe at Mrs. Sue's house, but somehow I thought my father would find me before Hamm got there to pick me up. If my father had found me, he probably would have beaten the hell out of me with his hands. He was just that mad.

When Hamm came, I felt safe. He took me back home, and my grandmother asked me what happened. I explained to her that my father was hollering and cursing at me. Of course, my grandmother didn't say anything, but to my surprise, my Aunt Denderant, who didn't like my father, said, "Who are you supposed to be? You're not too good to be hollered at." My grandmother said, "He doesn't have any business hollering at that boy, and he doesn't have to work over at the shop."

I knew my grandmother had my back.

"Go to your room and finish out your lessons (homework)," she said.

A couple of hours later, I heard the doorbell ring. When my grandmother went to the door, I heard my father say, "Hello, Mrs. Jones."

I didn't hear my grandmother say anything. My father said, "Is Goldwater home?" "Yes, he is here."

"May I speak to him, Ma'am?"

"If he wants to talk to you, he can, but if not, you can't see him…Garry, your father is here; do you want to talk to him?"

"Yes, I will talk to him."

My father and I went outside by the tree and talked. I could still smell the alcohol on his breath. The first thing that came out of his mouth was, "goddamn boy, you can run."

He said, "I'm sorry about what happened today; I want you to come back to work."

"I don't want to, and besides, I'm going out for the football team in a couple of weeks."

"You don't need to play any football. You need to work; are you coming back to work or what?"

I told him no and went back inside. I could tell my father was mad. He took this personally; we didn't speak to each other for about a whole year. He would see me on the streets and wouldn't say anything, nor would I. I can remember going on Queen Street to shoot pool; my father walked in and never opened his mouth to say anything. My cousin Eric would say, "Boy, there's your father; go say something to him." But I didn't; I just kept on playing pool, and wasn't doing a good job at that because Eric was kicking my behind and taking my money. After my father walked into the pool hall, I lost all concentration. It feels weird to see your father, and he doesn't speak to you.

Of course, my Uncle Hamm would be in the pool hall noticing everything that was taking place. He noticed that we weren't speaking. One of my friends named Vick, who hung out with my father, would say, "What's up, Gold?" I would shake my head as if to say, "Nothing much." It's ironic that even though my father and I weren't speaking, he would always show up for my sporting events.

When I was running Junior Olympics, I came to the bleachers to change my track shoes and saw my father. We both looked at each other, but we didn't speak. I spoke to Vick, a classmate of mine and a friend of my father's, but not a word was uttered to my father.

CHAPTER 19

My First Real Job

My first real job was probably in 1978 while I was still in eighth grade. The city had a summer program called Green Lamp. This program helped the youth of low-income families, ages fourteen and older, get summer jobs; it gave the children something to do and served as another tool to keep young people out of trouble. An idle mind is the devil's workshop, meaning if you don't have anything to do, then satan will put thoughts in your mind and convince you to get into trouble.

Most of the summer programs have been cut now; take notice of how more and more young children are getting into trouble. How can you expect young kids not to get into trouble when they don't have anything to do?

Out of all the government programs, why cut the summer job program for the youth? It appears that the government wants our children to get in trouble. Mayor Marion Barry (former Mayor of Washington, D.C.) was known for ensuring that the summer program for hiring young people was not cut. Once he went to prison, the new mayor came in and cut summer programs for the youth. What a dumb move! And it was a black mayor at that. She knows the plight of black youth, but then again, she may not have been part of the black struggle. It's hard for anyone to understand the plight of the black youth when they have never been in their environment; this includes our own black people. I'm not using this as an excuse because parents bear responsibilities as well. You have to know where your kids are located at all times. It's hard to do this with one parent, but this mission can be accomplished.

Getting back to my first job, when I was hired in the Green Lamp program, they assigned me to work at Caswell Center. This was a center for severely mentally challenged people. It was my understanding that the land Caswell Center was built on was supposed to have been for a university. As a matter of fact, this place was supposed to have been the home for East Carolina University. This should give you insight into how big Caswell Center is. I had been around mentally challenged people before, but not to this degree. We had a couple of mentally challenged individuals in Carver Courts that I became used to.

One of the guys lived behind me; his name was Clarence. Clarence was an older guy, around thirty-five to forty years old, with the mind of an eight-year-old. Clarence used to wear his dungarees and you would never see him without a Pepsi and a bag of peanuts. In fact, Clarence used to put peanuts in his Pepsi. It was easy to get Clarence wound up; all you had to do was tell him that someone was talking about his mother, Mrs. Briggs. Whenever the guys didn't like someone in the neighborhood or wanted Clarence to jump on them, we would tell him, "Hey man, Gino was talking about your mother."

Clarence would grab Gino by the collar and say, "I heard you were talking about my mother last year." Gino, scared as hell, would tell Clarence, "That was last year; why are you jumping on me this year?"

Clarence weighed around eighty pounds, but he was strong as an ox. Everyone was scared of Clarence. When he came at me with that bullshit about me talking about his mother, I'd tell him, "You can jump on me if you want to, but I'm going to tell my Uncle Hamm to whip your ass and go tell Mrs. Briggs." Little did Clarence know that I was afraid of him, but I couldn't let him know. I befriended Clarence just in case someone wanted to jump on me. First, I would buy him a Pepsi and some peanuts, and then he would settle down. Every day, Clarence looked for his Pepsi and peanuts, and sometimes he would grab at your pants pockets to see if you had any money.

"Damn, man, I don't have money every day."

He wasn't trying to hear that, but he wouldn't try to jump on me if I didn't have any money.

I recall this very special day involving him and my best friend, Antray. Someone told Clarence that Antray was talking about his mother.

"Look, Clarence, I wasn't talking about your mother; this isn't true."

Clarence wasn't going for it. Antray hauled off and knocked the hell out of Clarence, and it was on and popping then. After Antray hit Clarence, he took off running; Clarence was behind him, gaining ground. As I mentioned earlier, Clarence was about thirty-five to forty years old with the mind of an eight-year-old, and Clarence could outrun the average deer. He was chasing Antray, and the other guys thought he was going to catch him, but Antray was getting closer to home. The closer he got, the more Clarence gained on him; he was just one yard behind him. Antray's mother was at the door and saw Antray running toward the house to get away from Clarence. Antray's mother, Mrs. Christine (Rest in Peace) held the door open for him, and when he was just two yards away from the house, Antray dove in like a swimmer, and Mrs. Christine shut the door just as Clarence dove in after him. Clarence hit the door so hard that he knocked himself out. The guys were laughing their asses off.

To this day, I believe that after Antray hit Clarence, he didn't run from him anymore. I think Clarence was surprised that someone stood up to him. I understand that Clarence had been at Caswell Center at one time, but his mother decided she didn't want him out there, so she raised Clarence at home. Mrs. Briggs was determined not to give her child away because he was mentally challenged.

There was another mentally challenged brother in the neighborhood named Roosevelt. Roosevelt had some form of education; he used to ride the little yellow bus. This was a great thing that his family did; they cared enough about Roosevelt to get him some type of education. I think Clarence was a little more challenged than Roosevelt. Every mentally challenged person can't fit in the same category.

Roosevelt was a hustler like I was. He would sell bottles, rake yards, and do what he could to make money. Roosevelt could also count. In fact, today, Roosevelt is still doing the same chores he was doing in Carver Courts. Clarence is still being cared for by his sister in Virginia.

The last time I saw Clarence was at a family function. He can't see that well, but he's still wearing his dungarees and drinking Pepsi. I walked up to Clarence and asked if he knew who I was, and he said, "Yes." Clarence grabbed my stomach and shouted to everyone in the room, "Goldwater has a big stomach!!! Goldwater has a big stomach!!!"

Getting back to working at Caswell Center, I was hired around June 1978 and went for orientation the next week. I can remember my grandmother dropping me off for my first orientation. When she turned down Pecan Lane, I got excited because I knew I would be bringing home a nice paycheck and I would be able to help my grandmother. I got paid every two weeks, and I would give her half of my check. I didn't mind giving it to her considering how much she did for me.

The Caswell Center is located on Pecan Lane in Kinston, N.C. After the orientation, the supervisor who interviewed me told me I would be assigned to the Kendal Three or Kendal One building. When I reported to work, it was on and popping; the mentally challenged residents gave me a run for my money!

These residents were just like Clarence, but they were more challenged than Clarence and they were a lot stronger! On my first day, I was assigned to gather the residents together for lunch. This was a task because some would come to the table and some were out doing God knows what. My shift was 11 a.m. to 7:30 p.m. We had to be very careful dealing with the residents. Some were able to feed themselves, while others were not. During my shift, I was the only male working among a couple of females.

These females didn't have the strength to handle the residents, and who did they call on when some of the residents would go to fighting? Me, that's who—a 120-pound guy.

I was pretty strong myself, but the residents were three times stronger than I was. Some of them would get out of their chairs and cold cock the shit out of another resident; the resident that was hit acted as though he didn't feel a thing. After lunch we had to gather them for nap time, and this was a challenge because sometimes they would find a way to try to have sex with the female residents. And if they weren't having sex, they would go to the shower and masturbate. Seeing a mentally challenged person masturbate is a sight to see—working at Caswell Center, I had to encounter these types of things. If anyone tried to intervene while they were performing these acts, they had a task on their hands. One thing we must remember is that people who are mentally challenged have sexual arousals and feelings just like everyone else.

No one wanted to be the first person to stop the act because the residents would try to beat you down. I always hated when it was a full moon; the residents who were calm would suddenly get wild, and those who were already wild would become even wilder. Sometimes we would have three or four fights breaking out at the same time. When I grabbed one of them to take them down to the floor without trying to hurt them, I couldn't keep them down for long because they were slinging me off of them as soon as I took them down to the floor.

I would tell the nurse, "When I take them down again, I can only hold them for about ten seconds; you should be able to give them a shot of Thorazine in those ten seconds." After the Thorazine shot was administered, the resident's movements would slow down. After all the excitement, I would be drenched in sweat. There weren't too many days that I came to work and didn't work. Believe it or not, I enjoyed working at Caswell Center.

CHAPTER 20

My Sport Career Begins

I went out for the football team and made it. The position I played was quarterback. This was not street ball; this was organized sports. I wanted to be like my Uncle Jay because he played quarterback.

I had a strong left arm, but I didn't have the fundamentals down pat. Jay was the coach, and he would let me know that I didn't have the fundamentals right. When I ran the wrong play, Jay would embarrass the hell out of me by grabbing me by the helmet and pulling me toward him, fussing at me for messing up the play. I got so nervous that I messed up all the plays. The guys were laughing about this.

Jay was worse than Denderant on that football field. If you messed up, Jay made sure you knew. The same man who taught me to never allow anyone to take away my confidence was the same man who took it away in football. He always had a habit of restoring my confidence when we would ride home after football practice.

It's hard playing for a relative because they expect you to not make any mistakes, and they get on you extra hard because they don't want to be seen as showing favoritism. After practice, Jay would talk to me, and I would get my confidence back.

He said, "Gold, you got to be poised when you are playing quarterback because you are the leader. You can't be nervous, and you have to concentrate. I know you can get the job done. You have to stand in the pocket instead of running the ball." I didn't have any choice but to run because my line didn't block. Needless to say, I didn't get the job done because I was the second-string quarterback. All the games we played were away games, and I saw little action.

The season was fun because I loved traveling on the bus and joking with the boys. The guys would say, "Damn, Gold, you only got sixty seconds worth of action on the field. Your uniform is still clean."

Me (#5) and My Football Team, My Uncle Jay (Coach) is on the Far Right at the Back

After the football season was over, it was time for basketball season. Following basketball season, I tried out for the track team.

I had never run track before, so I didn't know what event to run. Coach Little and my Uncle Jay were the track coaches. When we had to report to practice, we had to run cross-country before we could start practice. I started off last and ended up last running cross-country. I was never a long-distance runner. It took me so long to run the cross-country that the team started practice without me. My Uncle Jay decided to give me a shot at running the 400-yard dash. That is one lap around a quarter-mile track.

I remember my first track meet. I asked one of my friends, "What is the best way to run the 400?" Mark was the fastest man on the team and one of Kinston's best running backs, in my opinion.

Mark said, "Gold, this is how you run the 400-yard dash. You start off slow, and when you get to the last one hundred yards, that's when you turn on your speed."

When the race started, I did like Mark said, and when I got to the 300-yard mark, I decided to turn on my speed, but the race was already over; I came in last. I never got any more advice from Mark.

In the future, Mark and I would become good friends, and we would run in relays together and set records. I ran the 400 yards in 63 seconds and that's when the coach started calling everyone who ran the 400-yard dash in over a minute "minute men." Before the year was out, I got my time under a minute; I think my best time was 58 seconds. I told the coach he could stop calling me a minute man. I really didn't like track because of my asthma, but I was a sports fanatic.

In my eighth-grade year, I got cut from the basketball team. I didn't do well in football or track. I started to give up on playing sports with the school team and go back to street ball, but I gave it one more shot the next year, and I never regretted it. This should be a lesson to kids: never give up, no matter what you do.

CHAPTER 21

Coming into My Own

I decided to go out for the freshman basketball team. I had gotten cut the year before. I was very hesitant, but I went out for the team anyway. I knew I could play basketball, but Kinston breeds basketball players; not everyone could make the team, and it wasn't because they couldn't play; it's just that the city of Kinston had so much talent in basketball.

When you hear of Kinston, you think about basketball greats. You think about people like Cedric Maxwell, former Boston Celtics MVP in the NBA Championship, Charles Shackelford, who played with many NBA teams, Mitchell Wiggings, Reggie Bullock, Jerry Stackhouse, who also played with several NBA teams, and now Brandon Ingram. We also had our football greats who played in the National Football League—Lin Dawson, Reggie "Supernat" Smith, Ronald Wooten, and Derek Rivers.

I remember when Langley High School came to town; this was the school Michael Jordan played for. The gym was packed. Michael Jordan used to put on a show, but he wasn't the only one putting on a basketball clinic. My cousin Herbert Suggs and my main man Vincent Lewis put on a basketball clinic as well.

When Jordan came down and dunked the ball, either Vincent Lewis or Herbert would come down and dunk it too.

Herbert Suggs Dunking the Ball - Photography Charles Buchanan (RIP)

Michael Jordan and My Buddy Vincent Lewis Goes Up For a Rebound During a Home Game at Kinston High School in Kinston, N.C. The Home of The Mighty Vikings! Photography Charles Buchanan

The Kinston High School coach used to put his best defensive players in to defend tongue-wagging Michael Jordan. There were more players who should have been in the NBA from Kinston, but either they didn't apply themselves or the coach didn't notify them of the college teams that were interested in them.

I remember being at a track meet, and my cousin Herbert was there. The opposing track coach wanted to know where he was going to school, and he said he didn't know. What Herbert didn't know was that the Kinston High basketball coach only gave him the names of the black colleges that were interested in him. This was a tradition with the basketball coach, and a lot of players missed great opportunities because of this coach. My cousin was able to go to Tulsa and play ball, not because of his basketball coach, but because of my Uncle Jay.

Uncle Jay and the eighth-grade basketball coach (Little) were responsible for most of the black basketball players getting into college to play sports. I can name all the great players that came out of Kinston High School, but there are too many to mention. The reason we played Michael Jordan's school twice a year was that they were in our conference.

Getting back to my basketball skills, I was quick with my hands, practiced hard, and could play defense. Coach Hamilton was the basketball coach as well as the driver's education teacher, and he would make comments when he saw me practice, saying "good defense."

"What's your name?" "Garry Jones."

This was a great sign when a coach wanted to know your name; this meant that they were interested or that you did something good to get their attention because there were a lot of people who tried out for the team that he didn't even know or care to know their names.

The first week went by, and the basketball team had their first cut. After practice, the coach said, "If I call your name, this means you made the first cut, and if I don't call your name, this means you can go home."

I think my name was the fifth name Coach Hamilton called. I was happy as hell, but it wasn't over. He cut about twenty-five players that day; he was trying to get the roster down to ten players. This left us with twenty players trying to make the team. Coach Hamilton would constantly say, "Good defense, Jones." He never said anything about my offense, even though I could play with the best of them.

I played point guard, and if I messed up the play, he would stop to tell me where I made my mistake. This made me think I wasn't going to make the team because I kept running the plays wrong, or someone else would mess up, and the point guard would be blamed for it.

Take for example, when you know you screwed up a play, you continue with the play. You bring the basketball back out at the top of the key and start the play over, but some jackass would tell the coach I messed up; hell, the coach knew that I messed up; he created the play.

This made me step up my defense game another notch; I knew the coach loved someone who could play defense. Whoever told the coach that I messed up the play, I would put my defense on them so hard that they couldn't get the ball across half court. I had the speed and quickness to do this. I even had the leaping ability to snatch a couple of rebounds and was strong enough to box you out.

I remember the coach giving me a compliment for boxing players out. I was about 5'6" at the time and was able to jump high enough to touch the basketball rim. The next week, the final cut came. I was nervous because I had made several mistakes. I remembered the compliment the coach gave me on defense, but at the same time, I remembered him telling me about the mistakes I made on offense.

Earlier, I mentioned that I was a point guard, but Dalton and Alonzo had that position on lock down. I knew that if I made the team, I would have to play behind those guys. After practice, the coach called us to the middle of the court and said, "I can only keep ten players. I wish I could keep everyone, but I can't. I have to let eight of you go, not because I want to."

Butterflies were in my stomach. I thought about being cut from the team last year and how it felt. I didn't want to feel that way again.

Coach Hamilton did the same thing that he did the week before. He said, "If I call your name, that means you made the team, and if I don't, this means you have to go home while I have a meeting with the team."

There were at least eight people that I knew of who were already going to make the team—cousin Herbert Suggs, Michael Fields, Alfonzo Jenkins, of course Dalton Frizzell (Sutton), Alonzo Rhem, the white guy Derrick Johnson, and Bo Kintz. I can't think of the names of the other guys that I knew who would make the team. I knew I had a very good chance, but I wasn't sure.

When the coach started calling names, it seemed like it took forever; the time just stopped or either it went in slow motion. The coach called the first eight names. These were the people who I knew were already on the team because they made the team the year before. Five of them started, and the other three got regular playing time. When the coach got to the ninth name, he called Tony Hill (Rest in Peace); he was my best friend in Carver Courts, other than Antray.

When the coach got to the tenth and final name, I started sweating. Coach Hamilton called the tenth name, and that name was Garry Jones aka "Goldwater." I said to myself, "Thank God!"

I really didn't want to celebrate because I knew some of the guys who didn't make the team, and I felt bad for them. After the coach selected who was going to play for him, he said a few words and congratulated us on making the freshman basketball team, telling us to meet him at practice at 4 p.m. the next day. Even though I felt bad for the others, I ended up going home to celebrate; this may have been one of the greatest moments in my life.

Me (#5) and My Basketball Team During My Freshman Year

When the season started, we all had guardian angels, but we never knew who they were. We knew they were cheerleaders, but who? The guardian angels would make us a food basket before every game…my guardians hooked me up!

As a matter of fact, during the whole basketball year, every week I got the biggest basket with the most snacks in it. Everyone wanted to know who my guardian angel was, but we didn't find out until the end of the season.

We only lost three games during the season, and I did get playing time; sometimes the coach would put me in when the other team had their best offensive player on the court. Whenever Tony Hill and I were in the game at the same time, I would pass the ball to him, or either he would pass it to me. I used to get the ball and take it through my legs and around my back, but I wouldn't shoot. When I would get home later that night, my Uncle Jay would say, "Gold, when you get in the game, you have to shoot the ball."

I pride myself on playing good defense. My girlfriend Nikki would be at every game, and when I got into the game, we would make eye contact. I wanted to make sure I did well because she was looking. I lost the ball out of bounds one time because I was too busy staring into the stands. We dated for about six months, and the relationship was great. I remember walking to her house during the holidays.

I didn't have a car, so I had to hit the pavement. I was weighing about one hundred pounds; whenever I would go to her house, her mother would always ask me if I wanted something to eat. Most of the time I said no; her family was really crazy about me. I stayed at her house until it got dark, and her mother made her oldest brother take me back home.

During the Christmas holidays, I didn't know what to get her, so I decided to ask my Aunt Mary, "What do you get a girl for Christmas?"

"Girls love to have a necklace."

I didn't have the money to buy the necklace, so my Aunt Mary bought me one to give to my girlfriend for Christmas. This girl was fine as hell; she was short with long, wavy hair.

She loved the necklace, and we both loved our favorite song by Barry White, "Just the Way You Are." Isaac Hayes had the same song out at the same time called "Don't Go Changing, I Love You Just the Way You Are." Our relationship would eventually break off because she didn't want to have sex; she was a virgin. She would always tease me like she was going to give me some, but she never did.

After the basketball season was over, I found out who my guardian angel was; her name was Sallie Davis. She made sure I had the most snacks in my bag. Sallie and I would become very good friends after that.

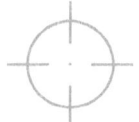

CHAPTER 22

Football and Track Season, 1979

Me Posing For an Individual Picture at Kinston High School

The football season came around quickly, and yes, I was still playing quarterback. My skills had improved, but not enough to be a starter. My confidence was up, but the first quarterback, Bo Kintz, had better poise than me, so he got the position. Although I did play during the season.

My knowledge of the position had grown a lot, but the blocking still wasn't there. The line didn't block when I came into the game, which forced me to run the ball a lot. This gave people the perception that all I wanted to do was run the ball, which was not true.

The 1979 football season came and went, and I can't remember how many games we won. In my ninth-grade year, I started dating again and met this girl; we both fell in love quickly. The only chance I had to spend time with her was at school.

Her parents didn't allow me to come to the house—or should I say, they didn't allow me to come in the house when I came over to see her. She and I did most of our dating at school. I can recall my first kiss with her; it made me fall even deeper in love. During exam times, I, she, and a couple of other people went over to my classmate's house and made love. She had on a red terrycloth short outfit. We were both kind of nervous because we were virgins.

Whenever her mother would put her on punishment, I wouldn't dare come over to her house. She wasn't able to use the telephone when she was on punishment. We both found ways around that. I used to have my sister Lisa call her house, and after Lisa talked with her, she would give the phone to me. When you are in love, you find ways of getting around things.

I knew when I walked her home, I would miss the school bus to take me home, but I didn't give a damn. After seeing her, the three-mile walk back home was a breeze because the only thing on my mind was the conversation we had just had.

I remember when Alicia and I were going to the Freshman Ball. The plan was for her mother to bring her to Kinston High

School, where the Freshman Ball was being held. I lived across the street from Kinston High School. Alicia was supposed to walk across the street to my house, and we were going to walk in as a couple. I had my corsage, and my grandmother was going to show me how to pin it on Alicia when she came over to the house, but she never showed up.

My grandmother kept asking, "Garry, where is she?" "I don't know."

I was embarrassed. I finally went over to the school, and the first person I saw at the Freshman Ball was Alicia.

"Why didn't you come over to the house?" "My mother wouldn't let me."

I told her, "I thought your mother had agreed to bring you over."

"I thought the same thing, but she changed her mind."

It was track season again, and this time, it was my breakout year. I was very good in the 400-yard dash; during the year, I only got first or second place. I was still dating my new girlfriend. We would walk each other to our lockers during class changes.

There was this one time when they called for the track team over the public address system to meet at the bus for an out-of-town track meet. My girlfriend and I were talking at the locker; she was there to wish me luck, when this other girl came up who used to like me and put her finger in my face, saying, "Garry, why didn't you call me back last night?"

I told the girl to get her fingers out of my face, but she didn't, and we started fighting. This girl put her fingers on the back of my neck and scratched the hell out of me; blood was coming down my neck. I was taught to never hit a girl, but my instinct to protect myself came out. The fight was broken up by other students, and we both went to the principal's office. The girl I was fighting, her mother was a school teacher at the same school. After her mother came to the office, she was told that her daughter had started the fight with me. After her mother saw my neck, she took her daughter out of the office and whipped the hell out of her. She told my grandmother she would pay for the doctor bill.

When I reported to the bus, my neck was burning, and I could feel the blood drying up. It was hot that day. My Uncle Jay had already found out what happened, and he told me to get on the bus; he would deal with me when I got home.

Needless to say, this was the first time I got first place in the 400-yard dash. When the gun went off to start the race, my neck was burning so bad that I couldn't wait to finish the race. I ran my ass off and got first place.

After we got back from the track meet, Jay and I went home, and Jay took off his belt and told my grandmother that I was fighting a girl. Before Jay could whip me, my grandmother said, "Garry doesn't mess with anyone; she must have been meddling with him, and he has the right to defend himself."

My grandmother saved me that day, and to this day, I have never fought another woman again. When I came back to school the next day, it was a tradition to announce over the public address system who had placed in the track meet. Of course, my neck was bandaged up, but when they called my name for taking first place in the 400-yard dash, I was happy.

During My Track Star Days

Having my girlfriend and receiving first place, I was in dreamland. Jay still had a leash on me; if my grades weren't up to par, in the summer of 1979, Jay put me on punishment and made me come in the house at 9 p.m. because I failed an exam.

"Jay, I was promoted to the tenth grade, and my grades were decent. Plus, I played basketball, football, ran track, and went to the Jr. Olympics all in the same year," is what I thought to myself.

I couldn't believe I was on punishment in the summertime. Of course, I didn't let the girls know I was on punishment, nor did I let the fellows know. I would come up with some lame excuse like I needed to be around the house at night because of my grandmother. My grandmother was fifty-two years old; she didn't need a man around the house.

I went on to run in the Jr. Olympics that summer. In 1979, it was a great year because I was in love, but at the same time, it was a hurtful year because I lost four people that I knew very well—Vince Davis (murdered), Curt Turnage (murdered), Rob Streeter (died of an illness), and Johnny Staten (died in a car accident).

CHAPTER 23

High School

In 1980, I went off to high school and got really into football and the rest of the sports. Alicia and I were still an item. I was playing junior varsity football; she would come to see me play. I was still the second-string quarterback, and Bo was still the first-string quarterback. Before practice, Alicia and I would meet somewhere private in the school and kiss before every practice.

When game time came, I was getting more action than I had the previous years, but the front line was not blocking. I remember when we had a home game and the coach told me to start warming up my arm; I guess Bo wasn't having a good game, and they put me in to play, mainly because my arm was stronger than his. Meaning, I could throw the ball further, but I could never get a pass off because I was always running for my life.

Roland Tate, who used to run the recreation center for Carver Courts, noticed what was going on. He told me that whenever I went in the game, the front line would step aside and let the defense come in on me. That's why I couldn't get a play off—before my center could snap me the ball, the defense was already in the backfield. This shit was getting political now, and Roland was the only one who noticed what was going on.

There came a time when I was able to get a couple of plays off. The first year, Michael Fields was my fullback, and Michael Pittman was my running back. Both of these guys were good. Pittman and I ran track together, and Michael Fields and I grew up together.

During the time that I was able to get a play off without running, Michael Fields was so strong he was taking the ball out of my hands! The play that was called was for me to fake giving the ball and pitch it to Pittman. Kinston High always ran that option. I loved this type of offense. It gave me an option to give Fields the ball if the hole was open, and if the hole wasn't open, it gave me the opportunity to pitch the ball to Pittman. Sometimes, the defense would get to me before I could pitch the ball to Pittman, and that's when I chose to run the ball myself—actually, I was forced to run the ball.

After the football season was over, Alicia and I's relationship was on shaky ground. Alicia was infatuated with older guys. She was popular, and everybody was trying to hit on her because of who her father was. We finally called it quits; actually, she called it off before I even knew it was called off. Someone told me that she had already started liking this older guy. This broke my heart. This was the first time my heart had ever been broken, and being with another woman was never the same because I started breaking their hearts. I had given up on playing basketball and concentrated on playing football and running track.

My 11th-grade year came around, and I had already become a track star. I was in all the relays, and from time to time, I ran the 100 and 200-yard dash. Kinston High's track team was loaded with talent. Fortunately, I was an asset to every relay team.

Track Team, First Row Center – Me, First Row Far Right End – Uncle Jay

Of course, I sat out of some relay teams to run individual events. When you run track, you could only participate in three running events and one field event. The school had a new track field, and the fans were coming out to see the track team. Track had gotten just as exciting as football and basketball.

When football season came back around, I was still playing quarterback, still behind Bo Kintz. My running back was Capp, and I forgot who my fullback was. I remember playing against Langley High School, the school Michael Jordan was attending.

The starting quarterback was Bo Kintz. Bo got hurt, and the varsity coach just happened to be at the game. The coach called me to go in the game to replace Bo. The play was a Green 23 option; the play was designed to fake giving the football to the fullback and pitch it to the running back. The team we were playing had already figured out how to stop the option. They had someone spying on the fullback, quarterback, and the running back.

When the play started, I couldn't fake giving the ball to the fullback because the defense was already in my backfield, so when I tried to pitch the ball to Capp, someone was already going toward Capp, and if I had pitched the ball to him, he would have lost yardage. So I tucked the ball away and ran for thirty yards.

When I went back into the huddle to call another play, I turned and saw Bo hopping back on the field. He said, "Gold, I came back to replace you."

I went to the sidelines and asked the coach, "What in the hell did I do wrong?"

"You did well."

"Well, why did you take me out of the game?"

He never answered my question. One of my friends, Jeff Jenkins, who was on the team, called me to the bench and said that he heard the varsity coach tell the JV coach to get me out of the damn game. He didn't want a running quarterback. I said to myself, "Fuck him, he is the varsity coach. Why is he controlling what the junior varsity team is doing?"

The next day in practice, the junior varsity coach told me that he was changing my position to wide receiver. I couldn't play quarterback anymore, and I said I quit the team. Football was my first love, and track was something I was good at, but I didn't love it.

I was still into the women; one of my friends named Capp said this girl named Cynthia Bailey liked me and wanted to talk to me, but Capp was lying. When I spoke to Cynthia, she showed no interest. I told Capp that he lied and that Cynthia didn't like me, and that's when Capp said, "Gold, I bet you can't get her to like you because she doesn't like underclassmen."

"If I really wanted her, I could pull her!"

After I started to talk with Cynthia, we began to like each other, but she was involved with another guy. But I kept after Cynthia, and eventually, we started dating. I had a lot of feelings for Cynthia, but not playing football weighed heavily on my mind.

The junior varsity coach came over to my house and told me he wanted me to come back on the team, but I couldn't play quarterback. This was not his decision; it was the varsity coach's decision. I gave in because football was my first love.

When I came back to the team, I wasn't starting at wide receiver, and I wasn't crazy about this. I had to earn the position. During the next game, I did earn the position because the coach put me in the game, and I scored a 50-yard touchdown pass the first time I touched the field. I started for the rest of the season.

Cynthia and I started dating really heavily, and the holidays were coming. I used to tell Cynthia about my dreams of becoming a professional boxer. One Christmas, Cynthia bought me some boxing gloves. When I opened my gift, I was excited. I took it home and showed it to Jay; Jay started joking, and Capp just happened to be at the house that day. Jay told Capp, "What kind of woman would buy her boyfriend some boxing gloves?" Capp said, "She must want him to go upside her head." Jay killed himself laughing.

Cynthia and I dated for about a year, and her family was crazy about me. I couldn't do any wrong in their eyes. My family was crazy about Cynthia; in fact, my family loved all the girlfriends I brought over to the house.

Going into my senior year, I was still playing football. We had a new coach with strict rules; he was a politician. In the summertime, most black players had to work, and they couldn't get to summer practice in the morning but made it to evening practice. They also didn't have cars, so they had to catch a ride to practice. Most white players had their own cars. This new coach wanted to kick them off the team; he wanted to know what was more important—working or coming to practice. He never considered that some parents made their children work during the summer.

I was blessed not to have to work during the summer, so I came to summer practice, but I still had to catch a ride. I was a great wide receiver, but I didn't start in my senior year. A junior started in front of me, and I believe the coach let him start because his father worked for the Kinston Board of Education. This guy didn't have the talent I had. It was politics, not racism, because the guy who started in front of me was Black.

It didn't last long because after the second game, I was starting at wide receiver. My relationship with Cynthia began to dissipate, and we would eventually break up. I ran one more season of track, and I got better and better. A lot of colleges were trying to recruit me. I'm not bragging, but I was a track superstar, and the whole Kinston knew about it. But the love for track still wasn't in my heart.

Women and football were my appetite. I remember hanging out on the block in Carver Courts; a guy named Turner was around and wanted to race me. He was an older guy who was supposed to be fast, but he had the nerve to want to race me in the streets. Another homeboy, Yogi, told Turner not to race me; as a matter of fact, Yogi put his money on me. I didn't have the money to bet Turner, but I knew I could whip him in running.

Turner and I got in the middle of the street by First Missionary Baptist Church and took off running. After the first ten yards, I smoked Turner, looked back at him, and started laughing… Yogi won his money, and I left the block.

CHAPTER 24

Heading to North Carolina Central University

I awoke one Sunday morning, and the phone rang; Jay was on the other end. "Gold, you ready?"

"Yes, I will be ready shortly."

I was ready to leave home, but when the time came for me to go to college, I had butterflies in my stomach. It wasn't like I was going somewhere I didn't know people, but being away from home on my own was something I had to get used to.

Jay and his wife, Debra, came by to pick me up to take me to the famous North Carolina Central University, two hours away from my hometown. Debra was an alumna of NCCU as well. We left Kinston and then stopped by Raleigh, N.C. to pick up my other mother, Mavis. She is my aunt, but most people sometimes call her my mother because she is always taking care of me.

She took on the responsibility of looking out for me since I was going to college. I had a nice mother named Mavis and a mean mother named Denderant—both were my aunts. After picking up Mavis, we headed thirty miles away to NCCU, the home of the Eagles that fly high and look low.

After we arrived, I said, "So, this is where I'm going to be." In my heart, I said, "I don't have any intentions of staying at this school, do I really want to go to school, or should I have gone into the military?"

My mind was going back and forth. I'm a grown man now, and I am responsible for every decision I make, whether it be good or bad.

When I arrived, it was alright, but when they left and waved goodbye, it wasn't a party; I felt empty inside. I went to the front lobby to pick up my room key. I said to myself, "I am actually on my own." I had money in my pocket and a lot of high school books that I could look at, yearbooks and stuff like that.

I went to my room, and one of my homeboys named Carlos Harris and my cousin John Grimes (Style Pooh) came and knocked on the door. "Come and go on the yard."

They knew it was my first time being away from home, on my own. They were seniors. They sensed that I was feeling bad; I was feeling bad because I missed home, but I was feeling happy because I was away from home. I had mixed feelings.

I left a support system. I left a program—home. What I mean by program is when you are home, you are programmed to do what your people tell you to do. That's just the bottom line. They tell you when to wake up, what to do, when you need to go out there and get a job, empty the trash, such and such. I didn't have that anymore, which was good, but I was surrounded by brand new people from all over the world. I left my grandmother, Tessie. I was glad that I left, but in a sense, I kind of wish she was there. I was hurt.

Shortly after or before I graduated from high school, I started dating this girl named Darlene. Then I broke it off because I didn't want a girlfriend. I wanted to be single, and anyway, Darlene was still in high school, and in order for me to concentrate on school, I needed to have my mind free.

When Jay and my two aunts got in the car to go back home, I grew up quick. Carlos, John (Cousin Style Pooh), and I went on the yard, and it was a different world. All of these damn women on this campus—I damn near went crazy. You meet different girls from all over the world, not just from a local city… a lot of international students at North Carolina Central University… it was sort of like Central was the mainstream; Kinston was local. I was meeting people from different walks of life that were sort of fun and exciting.

After I left the yard and returned to my room, another homeboy came over named Daniel; his room was located across the hall from me. Daniel said, "Where is your roommate?"

"I don't think I have a roommate."

We talked for a little while, then Daniel went back to his room. I went to sleep, and shortly after that, I heard someone with a key coming into my room. The guy said, "Get up."

This guy was about 6' 10" and played on the basketball team. His name was Cecil. He had his own apartment, but he also had a key to the room. He knew he had a roommate and that he was supposed to stay on campus because he was an athlete. He was on a scholarship, and athletes were supposed to stay on the yard.

"I just want to see how you were," he said.

"You're a big motherfucker, aren't you?"

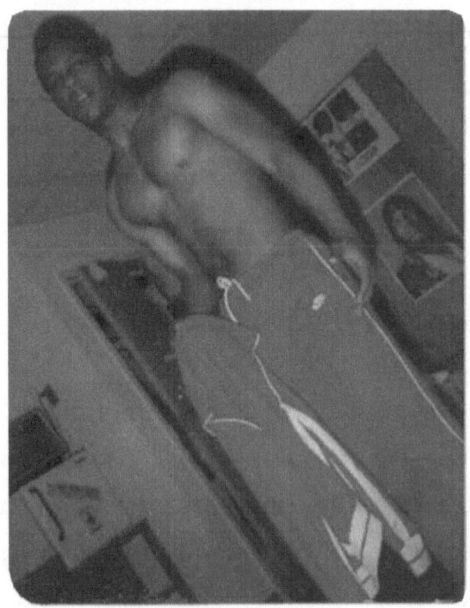

In My Room at College

I was still 135/140 pounds, but I was big and cut up. "Yeah, you look like you pump those weights... tell me about yourself, I'm Cecil."

He had a breathing problem just like I did; every time he spoke, he talked out of his nose.

He said, "Man, I am just here, and if anybody asks where I stay... I stay here. If the coach comes by, you just tell them I'm not here, but I stay here."

In all actuality, he wanted me to lie for him.

He said, "Anything you need, you let me know; I'll pick it up."

"What's in this refrigerator is mine...you buy shit, I'm going to eat it. If I buy shit, you can eat it. Oh, and I know about your homeboys."

Cecil used to take me over to his house; we used to chill out and talk. I started talking about how I was a superstar in high school and how I would have been a superstar in track here at Central because they really didn't have that many people running track at North Carolina Central as far as sprinters. I was probably the best sprinter out there besides Clarke, who would eventually go on to play with the Detroit Lions.

Cecil asked me, "Are you going to go out for the track team?"

"Yes, I am going to go out."

The real reason I really didn't get into that track team is that Kinston High had more than North Carolina Central had as far as track—better facilities. Being in college, you think you are going to have the best of the best, but then you get to college and realize you don't have shit. I had to prove myself to this new coach; I forgot the coach's name, but we didn't actually get along even though I had talent.

It wasn't like I thought it was going to be—becoming a track star. I thought I was going to have better facilities, and I realized

Central really only had a couple of guys coming out for track. They didn't even have enough people to put together a serious track team, and I was disappointed. This is a college, and when you make the team, they provide you with something. Hell, the coach wanted us to catch a ride with the kids that had cars to run at the University of North Carolina. I couldn't believe this!

```
                    UNIVERSITY OF NORTH CAROLINA
                            P. O. Box 3000
                          CHAPEL HILL, 27514

DEPARTMENT OF ATHLETICS                    HUBERT WEST, Head Track Coach
TRACK OFFICE                               DONALD LOCKERBIE, Head Cross Country Coach
(919) 962-5411


                            May 10, 1982


        MEMORANDUM

            TO:   North Carolina High School Track Honorees

            FROM: The University of North Carolina Track Staff

            We want to take this opportunity to congratulate you on your outstanding
            track and field performances so far this season. The 1982 track and
            field season in North Carolina has produced some very fine performances.

            We here at the University of North Carolina are in the process of putting
            together a very strong freshman class for the 1982-83 academic year. We
            have some of the top runners in the nation joining our program next year.
            We extend an invitation to you to be a part of this strong freshman class.

            If you would be interested in being a member of the 1982-83 University
            of North Carolina track and field squad, please fill out the enclosed
            questionnaire and return it to us as soon as possible. The enclosed
            brochure is for your evaluations of our program.

            Best wishes to you the remainder of this season.

                                            Sincerely,

                                            Hubert West
                                            Hubert West

                                            Don Lockerbie
                                            Don Lockerbie
```

University of North Carolina Invited Me to Join Their Track Team

I figured if you are on a track team, that means they are supposed to provide different things for you... a couple of guys had cars, and you had to get in with them to go over there. I was thinking being in college things would be more organized.

I thought they had money allocated for the track team, and that there would be a van or something.

I thought we would be able to get track shoes and stuff; we wouldn't have to pay for it like we did in high school because we are on the team. I really don't think North Carolina Central had the money. That program really went down because they were known for their track team when Dr. Walker used to be there. This track team didn't carry over that well.

Then I said, "I'm not running for free," and the coach felt like, "You haven't proved anything to me."

One of my friends, Frank, went to the University of North Carolina (I was offered a scholarship to run track for the University of North Carolina as well, but I chose not to accept it). Instead, I went over to North Carolina Central for a track meet just to see what Central had to offer.

Mr. Little, a track coach and 8th-grade basketball coach, and Jay (my uncle), the assistant track coach, also came up to see the college track meet. I had to catch a ride with someone else, and I wasn't running for Central.

When I went over there—I specifically remember it being a Saturday—the North Carolina Central coach was over there too. Herschel Walker was there running for the University of Georgia, and Kevin Bryant was running for the University of North Carolina.

I remember Kevin Bryant very well because he and my homeboy Ricky White were the fastest sprinters in North Carolina in high school. Kevin went on to play with the Washington Redskins. The North Carolina Central coach and my Uncle Jay had a talk.

Jay said, "My nephew isn't going to run for free. He doesn't have to prove his credentials; you can look at his record and tell his credentials are good, and he is a track star. You're not going to get him on that team and make him do this and do that; you're going to provide him with something, or he is not going to run for you."

Eventually, Jay said, "He isn't going to run at all."

Of course, I said, "I am going to do what Jay said… I'm not going to run."

I wasn't impressed with the coach anyway; that was sort of my excuse for not being able to run. Like I said earlier, my high school provided for us in track better than NCCU.

Me, Passing Baton in 400 Meter Relay

I'm not putting my school down because they are truly awesome now! It's just that track was not number one on the list of sports that the school put money into when I attended college.

They weren't providing me with anything; if I'm a superstar, you've got to provide me with things like my track shoes.

On the other hand, in a way I understood what the coach was saying, "You've got to prove something to me," but I had displayed all of the credentials out there for the coach to see—things I did in high school.

All of this took place in the fall. We had to practice in October to compete in indoor track. It was only a few months before trying out for the Central team that I participated in the High School State Track meet. I did all of this in May '82; we went out there and broke records. I say "we" because I was on the team that broke records—the 800-meter relay team and 400-meter relay team that broke records, new records.

This was just in the month of May; now we are talking about the fall (August). I hadn't lost that much ability; the new coach knew I had the potential to become a superstar at Central. I didn't have any problems running track for North Carolina Central, and I didn't have any problems being groomed by the coach, but damn, provide me with something. Needless to say, I never ran track for North Carolina Central University.

Speaking of playing sports, Daniel said, "Hey man, why don't you go out for the football team?"

"Why don't you go out for the baseball team? Hell, you were good in high school; as a matter of fact, you were a superstar."

"But you can run though, and we need someone from Kinston to represent us in sports," Daniel said.

The fellows really wanted to see me make it because they had gotten into the women; sports weren't on their minds. I was a freshman, and they knew I had talent—the same talent they had when they got to school, but they didn't take advantage of it. They knew if I made the football team, girls would come; not because you were a superstar, but just the fact that you were on the team.

Sports attracted women, and if a homeboy is playing, they could pick whatever woman they liked because the groupies love guys who played sports.

After Cecil and I had that long talk, the next day I went on campus to register for my classes. The lines were very long. I started to get out of line and say, "Forget college!"

This is the hardest thing you have to do in college—registering for those classes. I should have come to school a week early to register for my classes because you could take advantage of what classes you wanted. I learned real fast that the classes that I registered for were filled. It literally took a whole day to get the classes I wanted and to make sure my grant was valid.

I saw a lot of people who had to go home and come back the next semester because they didn't have a grant or their grant money was screwed up. Thank God when I finally got into the financial aid office, my name was on the register and there weren't any problems with my grant. I have to thank my aunt Denderant for that because she filled out all of my paperwork in high school.

After I finished registering, I ran into Daniel again, and he said, "Man, let's go down to Church's Chicken on Fayetteville Street and get three wings and a biscuit for a dollar."

Those wings were the biggest wings I had ever had—those wings must have had steroids in them, but they were good. After eating, we hooked up with Pooh and Carlos, and they introduced me to a couple of ladies, and the rest is history. I didn't need anyone to tell me how to talk to a woman. The only thing you had to do was introduce me, and I would take it from there. Sometimes, if I was interested in a woman, I would introduce myself to them.

After I left the fellows, I went back to the room, and the lonely feeling hit me again. If I wanted to make a phone call, I had to go in the hallway and wait in line to make a collect call. It's amazing when you go off to college how you start missing the little things that you were used to having; things like picking up a phone and calling whoever you wanted, taking a shower in private, looking at T.V. by yourself, and kicking it with your homeboys, like Antray and Capp.

It didn't take long for me to get a T.V.; I wasn't going to the lobby every day just to watch T.V. As far as friends were concerned, I was forced to make new friends. One of my best friends, Antray, was still in my hometown, and my other best friend, Capp, was attending Fayetteville State University. Capp always had a way to make things work to your benefit.

Capp would contact me with a calling card number, and I would use that calling card number to call long distance, although within a few days, the company would catch on to the fact that someone was using their calling card without permission, and they would cancel the card. Two days later, Capp would call me again with a new calling card number, and I would use it as much as possible until it was terminated. This went on for two years. One day, this girl named Norrece told me that the FBI called her house and asked her if she knew or spoke with anyone at North Carolina Central University. She told them, "No."

I guess she got scared and told them she didn't know what they were talking about. The FBI had caught on to this calling card scheme, and they were narrowing it down to catch the people who were using these calling cards. I remember Capp calling me and telling me the FBI came and got him out of class and took him to question him, asking him if he knew anyone from North Carolina Central University that he called. He told them, "No." The FBI was getting close, but the people I knew didn't snitch.

One day, in my criminal justice class, my instructor said, "I want to talk to you. The FBI wanted to know if I had a Garry Jones in my class. I told them 'yes.' They also asked me how you were as a student. I told them you are a good student. I don't know what you have gotten yourself into, but you need to quit."

The instructor told them when I would be attending class again, so I chilled from going to class for a few days. The FBI was waiting, but nothing ever happened after that.

CHAPTER 25

Falling in Love Again

Me a Few Years Later After Getting Into Weightlifting

I am going to be candid with you… I started building myself up, really getting into the weights because I had a surprise for everybody. I wasn't going to run track; I was going to try out for the football team, like Daniel suggested.

In November '83, I was pumping weights and thinking about trying out for this football team. I had met several females on campus, but it was nothing I was interested in. Yeah, I did a few things with those women, but I just wasn't in love with them.

In December of 1983, I started talking with this female from my hometown when I was home for the holidays. I was intimate with this female one time when I was in high school; this was right after she had gotten mad with her boyfriend, and she thought she was getting him back by being intimate with me.

Around Christmas time, the relationship had gotten a little more serious. She had just broken up with her boyfriend of many years, and we started our relationship even though she still had feelings for her former boyfriend.

I began to fall in love with her. When January of 1984 came around, I was still lifting weights and going home every weekend until I fell in love with Devita. She had a son already; he was about three years old. He didn't accept me right away because he was crazy about his father, but his father would never spend time with him. His father would call and tell Devita to have Derrick ready to be picked up on the weekends, but he would never show up or call.

Young Derrick

I can see Derrick right now, waiting by the door for his father, and when someone knocked, he would be very excited. But when I looked at his face, I saw disappointment. This kid was hurt.

This went on for a couple of months until Derrick stopped believing in his father, but he still didn't accept me. I don't care what I would do; he wasn't accepting me. I would read him bedtime stories before I went to bed, but even with this, I could tell he wasn't really in tune with me. I understood; to him, I was a stranger. Eventually, he started to open up.

Being that it was New Year's (January), my mindset was to still train and try out for the North Carolina Central football team. Each month passed by, and I was falling deeper and deeper for this woman. When spring of 1984 came around, I had to make a decision: either go out for the football team or just continue to come home every weekend.

I knew if I made the football team, I couldn't come home every weekend because I had to practice and go off to play games. The decision came easy: to hell with football, I couldn't stand being away from my girlfriend. I was whipped and didn't care. The fact that I didn't play sports made school not appealing to me; my attention was on my girlfriend and making money.

I stopped going to class, and my grades began to drop. I had made up my mind that I was going to go into the military and eventually get married. I remember going home and taking the army test. The guy asked me about my health, and I told him I had asthma. He said it probably wasn't a good idea to go in the military because I wouldn't make it through basic training. I told him I was used to asthma and had played sports all my life.

I took his advice and didn't apply, but my grades had already dropped, meaning that I received a letter at home about being on academic probation, and if I didn't bring my grades up, I would be suspended for a semester.

I remember being at home when I got the letter; I knew what was in it so I hid it. I think my grades had dropped to a 1.9, and when your grade point average drops that low, it takes a long time to bring it back up.

I knew I couldn't afford to make anything less than a C to at least bring my GPA up to a 2.5. I was in trouble and I knew it. I went to summer school to bring my grades up. I knew it was important to decide what I would major in because after summer school, I would be going into the fall as a junior. I had a pretty good idea what I would be majoring in, but it wasn't definite.

Going into my junior year, I knew my grades had to start improving if I wanted to graduate on time. I knew I had to start busting my ass in school because I came to the conclusion that majoring in criminal justice was best for me because every time I took a criminal justice course, I enjoyed it. I was an average student; I can't recall buying too many books while I was in school. I may have bought one or two during my time there; do you know what I used to do?

I made sure I went to school every day and didn't miss any classes; I made sure I listened really well because I knew I didn't have any books. I just took notes.

One weekend, I went home and asked my father if he could give me some money for my books. I said, "Man, I need some money to buy a book, you know, my school books."

"Man, I don't have any damn money; ask your damn mama." My mama didn't have any money to send me to purchase my books; I just said, "Forget it, I won't get any books. I'll continue to do like I had been doing, not buy any books."

I could tell my father felt like I was irresponsible because he had already given me a car, and someone stole it. He thought it was one of my friends who used to ride in my car. He felt like I let someone drive it, and they made a key and stole it. To top it off, my daughter Latoya was born, and I was still in school, and I had no way of supporting her. I said to myself, "This guy has some money; it's not like I'm asking for money to buy drugs or alcohol." I knew in order to go into my junior year, I needed some books because my grades were down.

Eventually, I would have to start buying some books. Sometimes my father could go into left field when you asked him for some money; he turned into another person. I was depressed, and now I had a child and didn't have money for books. My V.A. check hadn't come in when the fall quarter started, and I needed money for books. I said forget it.

Needless to say, I went back to school without money for books. Another reason I didn't have any money is because I was staying in an apartment; bills had to be paid, but having a child was my responsibility; 'I brought this child into this world, and it is my responsibility to raise it, and if a relative doesn't help, then I can't get mad at them.'

I decided to continue to pass the old-fashioned way. I went to class and took notes, and that's how I passed college—by taking notes. I had access to the money, but I just couldn't keep on asking my family. Colleen (Mavis) would have stepped up to the plate like she always does, but I didn't ask.

I was determined I wasn't going to ask her. Colleen sent me money all the time, but I didn't buy any books. The highest you can get when you don't have a book is probably a B or a C. But sometimes, when instructors teach, they don't just teach everything in the notes; there are certain things in that book that you are going to have to read that they are not going to go over.

I went to summer school and took a couple of Criminal Justice courses and made 2 B's. Then, the next semester, I made an A, 2 B's, a C, and 1 D; that kind of hurt because I couldn't afford to make a D. I didn't have the books, but I was still rolling... just imagine if I had the books. On second thought, even if I had the books, my grades still could have been the same; just because you have books doesn't guarantee you an A.

To be honest with you, in retrospect, the reason I didn't want to buy a book is because some of the things were hard for me to comprehend. I just hated spending forty or fifty dollars on a book trying to read something I didn't comprehend. To be able to comprehend early in life... you have to get in the habit of reading. Jay always preached that to me, "Gold, you have to read all the time."

Every now and then, I would borrow someone's book to read and give it back to them. Today, it bothers me that I was so blinded by love. I think I could have been a potential superstar, and I allowed love to stop me from pursuing my football dreams. I knew I could have been a superstar in track, but the passion wasn't there.

I never got into the athletic world the way I wanted to; I didn't even scratch the surface. The thing I enjoyed most about my college experience was being away from home; being able to drink, and go to parties. It was the end of my sophomore year, and it was time to get serious and find out what I wanted to major in.

You really don't get serious about your education until you're a junior. You needed to already have a major in mind and work toward that goal. Your first two years, you really don't know what you want to major in. I was confused…

I ended up saying, "I am going to major in Business because I heard other people say they were going to major in Business."

CHAPTER 26

He Crossed the Line

Prior to me going back to school for the fall semester in the summer of 1984, I went to visit my girlfriend one more time. It was the summer of 1984, and my girlfriend started facing financial problems; she got laid off her job. She had a gold Honda Accord stick shift that she'd taught me how to drive, but the car was being threatened with repossession.

I was working at Nova Center for my summer job, and I would ensure that I gave my grandmother her share of my paycheck even though I wasn't staying with her during the summer.

Of course, I would go by the house every day and eat her good cooking, and when I would get mad at my girlfriend, I could always go back home. I would go home in the middle of the night, fall asleep on the couch, and the next morning, when I awakened, a blanket would be over me, and I could smell that good ole fashioned bacon, grits, and eggs.

My grandmother would say, "Garry, breakfast is ready," and I would say, "I will be in the kitchen in a minute."

Every dime I gave to my grandmother, I never regretted. My grandmother would bend over backwards to ensure I had everything I needed. I could tell she wasn't comfortable with me cohabitating (shacking). During that time, I felt like I was grown, but in my grandmother's eyes, I was never grown.

After giving my grandmother a portion of my paycheck, I tried to help my girlfriend with her bills. I really didn't want her car to be repossessed because I was driving that car to work most of the time.

One summer afternoon, my girlfriend left the apartment and said, "I'm going downtown to try to borrow some money from this financial company."

I told her, "If you do borrow some money from them, it's going to take forever to pay them back because they have the highest interest rates in the world."

My girlfriend was never lazy; she had always been independent. As a matter of fact, I never dated a woman who was dependent on me. She was excited about going to borrow the money. One thing about a finance company: you may have bad credit, but they would lend you the money, and when you finish paying the loan, you would have paid at least five times over. An hour later, she walked back in the house without a smile on her face.

"How did it go? Did you get the loan?"

"No, I didn't get the loan."

Of course, she had been turned down for a loan before, but this time her demeanor was different. Normally, when she would get turned down for a loan, it wouldn't bother her, but I could tell something was wrong; she was holding something inside that she didn't want to tell me. She knew I was about half crazy, so therefore, she couldn't share everything with me. I insisted on asking her what happened downtown at the loan office.

"Garry, I don't want to discuss it."

"Woman, what the hell do you mean you don't want to discuss it?" I asked angrily. "Tell me what in the hell happened at the loan office!"

"Garry, if I tell you, promise me that you are not going to snap."

"What am I going to snap over? I'm calm, now tell me what the hell happened before I snap."

"See, you are already getting mad before I can tell you what happened."

"I wouldn't be getting mad if you would have come out and told me what happened. You were beating around the damn bush."

"Garry, the man said I could be approved for the loan if I come back at 5 p.m. after the office was empty and go to bed with him."

"What did you just say?"

"Garry, you said you weren't going to snap."

"Come on, let's go. Get the damn keys, and let's get the hell out of here! Take Derrick over to your mother's house and let's go back downtown to the loan office. I'm getting ready to straighten this old bastard out!"

"I'm not going anywhere with you; if you want to go downtown, you are going to have to go by yourself."

"Oh hell no, you are going if I have to snatch your ass and put you in the car; you are going!"

She could tell by the way I was getting angrier that I had lost control. I grabbed the keys and told Derrick to get ready because he was going over to his grandmother's house, and me and his mother were going downtown to take care of some business.

She knew I couldn't drive the stick shift that well, and she knew I didn't like to drive in traffic with the stick shift, but I was so mad that I didn't care if the car cut off every second. I was determined to go downtown. We dropped Derrick off at his grandmother's house and proceeded to go downtown. She refused to drive, but I didn't care; the car continued to cut off as we were leaving.

While on the way, we argued back and forth. "If it's not bothering me, why is it bothering you?"

"Look, woman, you just don't let anyone disrespect you like that and get away with it!"

"I knew I shouldn't have told your stupid ass anything; men are going to be men, and you shouldn't let that bother you! You are burning my clutch, you need to change gears!"

"Don't tell me how to drive this damn car! The car is going to be torn up by the time you get there."

"The hell with what you are talking about! Don't try to change the subject. White people think they can talk to Black women anyway they want to, and the Black women always ignore it! This is not slavery, and you are my woman. No one is going to disrespect you. If you don't stand for something, you will fall for anything!"

As we approached the loan company, I found a parking space, but I had to parallel park, and that was hard when you weren't used to driving a stick shift.

I said, "The hell with the parallel parking; I'll just find a parking space that I can just drive into without keeping on shifting gears." When I parked the car, she refused to get out.

I said, "If you don't get out of this car, I'm going to snatch you out!"

She agreed to get out of the car. When we went inside the loan company, I saw my homegirl in the corner typing. She was working for the loan company. When my girlfriend and I approached the desk where the loan officer was, this white old man came out and said, "Oh, you are back again."

He had a smile on his face when he was talking with my girlfriend. I informed the loan officer that I was the boyfriend and that my girlfriend said you could get the loan if she came back at 5 p.m. and had sex with you.

"Sir, this must have been a mistake; I would never say anything like that."

I grabbed that loan officer by his necktie and brought him closer to me, told him that he was lying, and if he didn't apologize to my girlfriend, I would break his damn neck. That man turned redder than blood. I refused to let him go because I was still mad. He apologized, and my girlfriend said, "Garry, let him go!"

While still holding the man by his tie, I told him that my grandfather was the President of the NAACP chapter of Kinston, and he is the Vice President of the NAACP chapter for the state of North Carolina, and I would have that financial office closed down.

After I let the man go, my girlfriend and I left. I told her we were going to the police station to file a report. She was reluctant, believing that his apology was sufficient. I didn't care about him being sorry; he was going to pay for his conduct.

She wanted me to leave the situation alone and return home; I was not leaving anything alone. When I spoke to the captain of the police department and informed him of what had happened, he stated that he could charge the loan officer for solicitation.

The captain said, "I want your girlfriend to wear a wire, and when she goes back in the office for the loan, we can trap him."

I said, "I don't think that man is going to fall for that; I've already told him what I was going to do to him if this shit happens again."

The captain said, "You should have let us handle this situation; we could have gotten him."

We left the police station and argued all the way back to the apartment. We were still behind on the car payment, and we didn't want repossession on her credit. One of the guys in the neighborhood had heard about Devita trying to get rid of her car; he heard about this through my girlfriend's brother.

He came by the apartment and said he wanted to put $500 down on the car and take up payments. He said he was going to the beach with his fiancée, and he would have the money the next week. We agreed that this was the right thing to do.

Later on that evening, while looking at the news, a special report came across: "Man Drowns at Beach—coming up after the commercial." When the news came back on, I recognized my homegirl being interviewed. She was crying and said she and her fiancée were in the water at the beach, and when she turned around, she couldn't find him anymore—he went under the water and never came back up; he got caught in a current. The man that drowned was the same man my girlfriend and I agreed to sell the car to. This was a tragic story; the car was repossessed, but my homegirl will have to live with her fiancée drowning for the rest of her life.

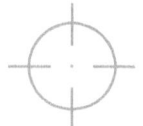

CHAPTER 27

The Classic

It was the summer of 1984 when I first moved into my apartment while attending North Carolina Central University. I needed transportation and would always ask my father if I could have one of his cars; the one I wanted was the 1965 Buick Convertible.

My father wouldn't drive that car unless it was on the weekends, mainly Saturdays. He would have his dog, a Doberman Pinscher, riding on the hood of the car just cruising around Kinston. I had told him a year ago that I wanted that car, but he just shrugged me off, saying I couldn't handle it. I would always say, "Yes, I can."

Anyone who knew my father knew he drove a hard bargain. He wasn't going to give you anything, but those who knew me also knew I wouldn't stop until I got what I wanted. I think this was the first time my father ever gave in to me when I wanted something. I worried him like crazy.

One day he called me up and said to come get the car. Of course, when I got the car, I had to hear a sermon from my father. Sometimes I think he missed his calling; he should have been a preacher with all the sermons he gave.

"Goldwater, I don't want you having a lot of people riding in this car."

"Okay, I understand. Could you give me the keys?" I wanted those keys badly.

"Hold up, Goldwater; let me tell you more about this car before you go jumping in it."

He could tell I was excited. After going over a few details about the car, he finally handed it over. To be honest, the only thing I wanted to know about the car was how to let the convertible top back. I had already envisioned what I was going to do. My mind didn't think about the mechanics of a car; I guess because my father was a mechanic, everything had already been taken care of, and it was. As long as the car cranked, that was the only concern I had. I had a lot of good times in that classic.

1965 Buick Convertible

Me and Pete on His Car – Classic in the Background

I used to drive up and down the highway, back and forth from Kinston to Durham, N.C. When I came home to see my girlfriend, I would leave late going back to college on Sundays. My Aunt Mavis always advised me to leave early to avoid any issues in case the car broke down on the highway when it was dark. I didn't think my car could break down; I had the best mechanic in the world working on it—my father.

The average person looking at my car would say it was old, and the first thing that crossed their mind was, "I wouldn't take it out of town." When it started getting dark, my Aunt Mavis would tell my grandmother, "You need to make Garry get on the highway. It's getting dark, and he doesn't need to be on the highway."

I think what my Aunt Mavis told my grandmother fell on deaf ears because my grandmother didn't say anything to me. I was a grown man and could make my own decisions; I would never disrespect my aunt in any way. But I must say, my grandmother was a good listener and didn't always say what her children wanted her to say to her grandchildren. I miss her very much!

CHAPTER 28

Classic Memories

I guess you're all wondering why I called my car, The Classic. I can't remember who named the car—maybe it was my friends, Poonie, Antray, or Capp. I do know my father said that after twenty years, your car becomes a classic, and after twenty-five or thirty years, it's considered an antique. But nevertheless, the name of my car was The Classic. The Classic had some very exciting moments in some very exciting towns with some very exciting people riding in it.

I can recall one classic memory: my homeboy Delmus Brown (Poonie) came to see me at North Carolina Central; he stayed with a friend of his family in Durham for a couple of months. In reality, he spent more time in my room on campus than he did with his brother. He got a job in Durham working in an upscale restaurant named Alexander. Most of the people who came to eat there were wealthy. I remember Poonie telling me that the hamburgers were some ridiculous price, like $25, and the uniforms they had to wear were a black tie, white shirt, and a blazer. Whenever I didn't have money for gas, Poonie would take out his tip money and supply The Classic with gas. Sometimes Poonie would bring back $75 in one night from his tips.

One day, after Poonie came from work, he wanted to go over to the University of North Carolina to party. I told him that I couldn't make it. He said, "Chuck, I've got the money for gas." For some strange reason, he started calling me Chuck. As a matter of fact, we both started calling each other Chuck from time to time. "It's not that I don't want to go, but I have a term paper I have to turn in by tomorrow in Psychology." "Where is your book?" Poonie said. "It's in the corner."

Poonie got the book and turned to the chapter I was supposed to be studying to write the term paper. He grabbed a tablet and an ink pen, and within 45 minutes, the paper was finished. An hour later, we were on our way to the University of North Carolina in Chapel Hill to party. We had another homeboy named Gerald who rode with us to Carolina. He provided the drinks and the weed, and before we knew it, we were on Country Club Road trying to find Great Hall on the university campus where the college people partied.

I didn't smoke weed that much because it made me paranoid; I didn't like putting anything in my body that made me paranoid. I did drink the hell out of some Cognac called Courvoisier, and when we got to the party, we were already high. We had a great time in a great city.

When we arrived back at North Carolina Central, I took a shower and got ready for class the next morning. My first class was Psychology. I turned in my term paper, and a couple of days later, my instructor returned it to me with an A. I was happy!

By this time of the year, it was close to North Carolina Central's Homecoming. Normally, I had friends from Kinston and other universities joining in the festivities.

I can recall one of my friends, Kelvin Edmonson (Capp), coming to town for homecoming. He caught a ride from Fayetteville State University. I told him I would take him back that Sunday after homecoming, and he was down. When Sunday came around, I told Capp that I wanted to leave in the afternoon to take him back to Fayetteville State University because I wanted to be back in Durham to attend class Monday morning. Fayetteville State was only an hour and a half away. Poonie, Capp, and I got up Sunday afternoon, helped Capp put his luggage in the car, and went to the gas station to fill up The Classic, heading off on one of the craziest times I ever experienced in that car.

"Capp, you can drive because I need to study for a test in the back," I said. We had gotten about forty-five minutes outside of Durham when we heard a loud noise. Capp almost lost control of the car! I didn't know what was going on. Capp pulled to the side, and we realized we had a blowout. We changed the tire and headed on our way to Fayetteville, but fifteen minutes later, we heard another loud noise. "Not another blowout!!"

We knew we were in trouble then because we didn't have another tire and, like always, had little or no money. We were in the city of Fuquay Varina. It was kind of warm that day, and we knew we would somehow get help. We sat in the car and joked for a while, then the sun started going down. Most businesses were closed. There was some old wine under the driver's seat of my car; it had been there since my father first handed it over to me. We got thirsty and drank the dinner wine, realizing we needed help soon.

A woman stopped by. "What's wrong?" "We have two tire blowouts and need a tire and a rim to put on the car." "Are you college students?" "Yes." "Do you have any money for a tire and rim? This could be pricey." "We have $15." "That is not going to be enough. Wait here until I return; I'm going to find someone to help."

We got in the car; it was getting darker and started getting cold. Twenty minutes later, this lady came back with a man named Pork Chop. "Pork Chop, these are the students I was telling you about; they only have $15. Now, what can you do to help them because they need to be back in school by tomorrow morning?" Pork Chop looked at the size of the tires and said, "Since they only have $15, I'll have to go to a junkyard I know and try to find a tire and a rim that fits their car. Let me see what I can do." "I'll stay with the students until you get back." "Okay." We started small talk with the lady, and about an hour later, Pork Chop came back with a tire and a rim. We all started smiling because we knew God had answered our prayers. We gave Pork Chop the $15 and told them we appreciated what they had done for us and that we would find them to pay the rest.

The lady said, "You don't owe us anything. You all drive safe and keep your grades up." Poonie, Capp, and I finally made it to Fayetteville, N.C. Capp told me to stop at Church's Chicken so he could use the bathroom. "I need to use the bathroom too."

When Capp and I came out of the restroom, Poonie was in line ordering a couple of pieces of chicken and two biscuits. "Poonie, where did you get money from?" "Out of my socks."

"What do you mean you got money from out of your socks?" "I always keep money in case of hard times." I said, "We could have given that money to Pork Chop for helping us out…Man, you and Capp get a piece of chicken and a biscuit."

"How much money do you have?" "Man, I only have $5; by the way, I'm hungry. Shit, we all were hungry." That was the best piece of chicken we ever had. After dropping Capp off at his dorm, we headed back to North Carolina Central. I arrived late.

Needless to say, until this day, we never went back to give Pork Chop the money we promised him. Our intentions were good; we kept saying we would go back when we had more money, but it never happened. I wonder what Pork Chop and that lady are doing today. I would love to see them again.

CHAPTER 29:

Deciding My Major

Studying During My College Days

Finally, decision time; it was put up or shut up! I had to make a choice; at first, I didn't know what I wanted to study or what I wanted to do. I wasn't a bit more business-minded than the man on the moon. I just said that because someone else claimed it was their major.

I remember earlier in my sophomore year, I took Intro to Criminal Justice as an elective course, and all of a sudden, I was able to comprehend what I was reading. A light bulb went off in my head, and I said, "I like this." The reason I liked criminal justice was that I could comprehend crime since most of my friends were criminals. I could relate.

When the subject of probation and parole came up, I knew a lot about it because the guys in Carver Courts I used to hang with were going back and forth to jail, then getting out on parole. Criminal justice interested me because of the criminals I knew. I used to hang out with the crooks until they went out and committed a crime. I had the sense not to go along, but they would give me some of the items they stole. I could have been locked up for receiving stolen goods. I learned this kind of language not through books and Intro to Criminal Justice, but growing up in Carver Courts.

Anyway, that's how I got into Criminal Justice. That's when I started getting educated and forming some type of idea of what I was going to do. My major was Political Science, and my minor was Criminal Justice. On top of all the pressure of deciding my major and getting my degree, my daughter LaToya was born, and she was my responsibility.

I started going home every week because I wanted to be more than a father; I wanted to be a man that stuck by his girlfriend during her pregnancy. It's easy to get a woman pregnant, but can you stand by the woman when she is actually carrying your baby, losing her shape, and dealing with the mood swings?

My Daughter, LaToya, and I

I was the man for the job because of how I was raised. It wasn't easy, but I got through it and made my grandmother proud because I was taking care of my responsibilities. I'm not saying my grandmother was happy I got someone pregnant while in college and unmarried; I'm just saying she witnessed the child she raised stepping up to the plate and handling his responsibilities.

Some men run from this responsibility, but I embraced it. After LaToya was born, I thought my party days were over, but not quite. Criminal Justice became easy for me, so I didn't have to study as hard. I used to get in my blue 1965 Buick convertible. The boys and I used to go over to the University of North Carolina and party.

Off to My Intern Job as an Adult Probation and Parole Officer

The University of North Carolina was only twelve miles from Durham. I used to see Michael Jordan all the time because he went to school there and would come on the yard at North Carolina Central to party with us. He would go straight to the student union to get his hair cut until he started shaving his head bald. I didn't know Jordan personally, and I'm not going to sit here and lie and say, "Hey man, I used to party with Michael Jordan, and we were buddies." I didn't know Mike, and he probably didn't know me from Adam and Eve. We spoke a couple of times in passing.

He was always a nice guy, and I can honestly say I never saw Jordan with a beer in his hand, but I did see other athletes who eventually made it big in the professional leagues getting real wild at parties. If Jordan were to see me today, he probably would say, "This guy looks familiar, but I can't say that I know him." Michael Jordan was always professional every time I saw him. When I tell people we played against Michael Jordan, they don't believe me, as if Michael Jordan just dropped out of the sky to play professional basketball.

First and foremost, Michael Jordan was born just like everyone else; he went to school just like everyone else and played sports. He is from Wilmington, North Carolina, which is only an hour from Kinston, North Carolina, the place where I grew up. I used to have a homeboy that threw wild parties in Chapel Hill; he had everything most people wanted at parties, from beer to drugs. I used to see some famous athletes there indulging, but it was all good; at least they weren't fighting. But I can honestly say I never saw Jordan do anything illegal.

Whenever I drove my 1965 Buick Convertible over to the parties, I had another homeboy traveling with me. He was what I would call a male groupie; he loved to go to parties with his weed. He sold a little weed himself and would love to go around famous athletes and let them get their weed for free just to say he smoked weed with this athlete. These guys used to use Fred, and they loved riding in the convertible.

Those days are long gone. I'm not trying to down any athlete or anything like that, and I don't want to mention any names as to who was doing what, but what I will say is, "Michael Jordan was the model athlete in North Carolina during my time."

CHAPTER 30

Getting in a Fight at the University of North Carolina

I was still partying in school. One particular night, I went over to the University of North Carolina for a party and met Carlos. He was a homeboy.

This football player from the University of North Carolina made a mistake and stepped on Carlos's shoes without apologizing. I can't think of the guy's name, but he went on to play professional ball. Carlos asked the guy, "Do you wear the same size shoe that I wear?" I guess the guy didn't understand what Carlos was saying. Hell, I didn't understand what Carlos was saying either. Carlos always came out with that D.C. slang.

The guy asked, "What are you talking about?" "Motherfucker, you stepped on my shoes and didn't apologize!" An argument began, and it got real heated. Most of the University of North Carolina football players came over to help their teammate out. It was just me, Carlos, Poonie, and my cousin Pooh, who were at the party from Central. We couldn't fight the entire University of North Carolina football team by ourselves; those guys were big as hell.

When the whole football team surrounded us, I told Carlos, "You need to chill; we are on their turf." Carlos had been drinking and didn't care. We got Carlos out of the party and went back over to Central. I can recall another incident Carlos and I were involved in when we went to Washington, D.C. He advised me not to say anything to the Prince George County police or the Fairfax County policemen; they would lock you up fast.

After going to a couple of Go-Go clubs and drinking, things went bad. I think we first went to a club called Chapter 3 located in D.C.—a big fight broke out. "Man, I'm ready to leave this club." "Well, let's go to the Gold Room to party. I think the group 'EU' or 'Rare Essence' was playing there that night, and when those guys get on stage, they play for about five hours straight and the people dance for five hours straight. Washington D.C. created the Go-Go, and the father of Go-Go is Chuck Brown." After we left the club, Carlos suggested that we go to I.H.O.P. (International House of Pancakes) for something to eat. Carlos got into an argument with the same policemen he told me not to say anything to because of their reputations for beating people up.

I had to use the bathroom real bad, so I went to the bushes to relieve myself. The policeman came over to arrest me for using the toilet outside. Carlos stepped in between us and said, "Man, he wasn't doing anything but using the restroom." I think the policeman told Carlos to stay out of it; then Carlos and the policeman got into an argument. I thought they were going to beat Carlos down. After all, they did have a reputation for beating up black men, especially in Fairfax County. Those white policemen would beat you down and not think anything of it.

Eventually, I apologized to the policemen, and we went into I.H.O.P. and ate until our high came down. I think we drank a little too much alcohol that night. Every time I see Carlos now, we talk about what happened. The next day we drove back to North Carolina and made it back just in time for my 9 a.m. class. Since I didn't have any books, I couldn't afford to miss any classes. I had another roommate named Coleman, and I'm glad he didn't make that trip to D.C. with us because when Coleman starts drinking, you know there's going to be some mess since he could never hold his alcohol. You either had to pray or get away from Coleman when he was drinking. Those were the only two options. The funny thing about Coleman is that he couldn't remember anything the next morning.

CHAPTER 31

The Night Coleman Flipped

I haven't talked about Coleman much in this book, but boy, he was something else. Coleman was my roommate when I moved off campus. He was about ten years older than me—a homeboy with a history in Kinston, and that history was his drinking. Coleman was a very good person; it's just that he turned into another person when he drank alcohol. Ten years before I got to North Carolina Central University, Coleman had attended it as well, just like many homeboys. Most of them dropped out and stayed in Durham, North Carolina.

When I arrived and started school, Coleman said, "Man, I can't believe you're in college already. I'm going back to finish up those hours I dropped out for because I'm not going to let you get your degree before I do, boy. I raised you."

Everyone loved to say they raised me. I told Coleman, "I'm looking forward to moving off campus." "We can be roommates," he suggested. "I'm down."

We got an apartment on Fayetteville Street called Parkview Apartments. Coleman and I had a two-bedroom place. We didn't have any furniture, so I got my mother's couch, a recliner from storage, and an old coffee table. I didn't have a bed; I slept on the couch or a sleeping bag. Coleman was working at the Durham County Library at the time. It just so happened that we lived only one door down from where Coleman and the Kinston crew had lived ten years earlier. We had a lady named Aretha living in the apartment above us; she was our mother away from home. She had been living in Parkview when Coleman lived there a decade earlier. Our apartment was always packed; all of our homeboys used to come over. Sometimes you couldn't tell if you were in Kinston or Durham. Weed was getting sold out of that apartment. I wasn't into the weed, but I was drinking Budweiser or Private Stock Beer; I've already mentioned the liquor I drank—Courvoisier.

I knew Coleman was selling weed, but he tried not to do anything in front of me. He would always take his customers to the back, or if I were in my room, he would take care of business in the living room. My attitude was, "He can do whatever he wants as long as I'm not a part of it." He used to always say, "Gold, if something happens to you, your Uncle Hamm told me he would kick my ass."

Once during homecoming, Coleman got so messed up that when we left for the homecoming show, he said he would meet us there. We had visitors from out of town staying with us; anytime anyone from Kinston came to visit, our spot was where they'd come.

We had our tickets to see the O'Jays, Mtume, and Chaka Khan. When the other homeboys and I went to the show, we left Coleman at the house with a beer in his hand and a joint in his mouth. Chaka Khan was looking so good at the show that I told one of the homeboys, "I have to go backstage to meet her," especially when she broke out and started singing "Sweet Thing."

I proceeded to go to the back of the stage; I got through the first rope without being stopped. When I got to the second rope, security said, "You can't go backstage."

Antray was visiting at the time and told me, "Let's go back to our seats." Antray and I had always been the best of friends. After the show, we went everywhere and to all the parties. We never saw Coleman at the show. We thought maybe we didn't see him because it was so crowded.

When we got back home around 5 a.m., I stuck my key in the door; Coleman was laid out on the couch with his show ticket in hand. He had passed out from drinking too much.

I will never forget another time when we had a homeboy stay with us for about two weeks; his name was Bud. He sold weed back in Kinston.

One evening, when Coleman got off from work, his income taxes were in the mail. The next day, two more homeboys came by and said let's go to a club. I forgot to mention the bottle of Hennessy Coleman brought home. We all drank, and as you know, I couldn't smoke the weed.

Anyway, we decided to go to this new club in Raleigh, North Carolina, named Club Raleigh, owned by this big guy who played in all those movies like Training Academy. In the movie, he was the biggest black guy with the police officer uniform on.

When we walked in the club, the owner was at the door; we paid and went to the upstairs area. Our homeboy Los thought we were in Kinston; he took out some weed and proceeded to roll a joint. We had to tell Los that this was not the Club back in Kinston. This was a top-notch club; he needed to put that away. Of course, we had all been drinking before we got there, but Coleman's other personality hadn't come out yet. It only came out when he drank beer and liquor.

When the waitress came around to take our drink orders, Coleman said he was paying for all of us. It was just four of us, and Coleman was beginning to allow his second personality to emerge, but even with this, he knew how to count his money. I don't care how drunk he got; it was hard to cheat him. When the lady got back with the drinks, she started counting Coleman's money back to him. When she was counting, she told Coleman it was a ten-dollar bill; she was really giving him a one-dollar bill. Coleman knocked all the drinks off the tray and said, "Bitch, you trying to cheat me!"

That's when all hell broke loose. The bouncers came over and grabbed Coleman; I told one of them, "Let me handle him."

"If you don't get control of him, we're throwing his ass out of the club."

I told Coleman, "Calm down."

"I'm not calming down; that bitch tried to cheat me!"

One of the homeboys and I went downstairs to dance. Before we knew it, we looked upstairs and saw a lot of commotion; then we saw Coleman. We ran from the dance floor to get to him.

When we got upstairs, the bouncers already had Coleman in the air. Coleman wore glasses, and half of them were hanging off his face. I told the bouncer, "Let me take him home!"

"No, we are kicking him out!"

"I agree that he should be out of the club, but let me take him out!"

I knew they were getting ready to beat Coleman's ass. One of the bouncers pushed me back.

"I'm not Coleman; I am just as big as you! If you put your hands on me again, we will be fighting! I am trying to bring peace by taking Coleman out of the club."

As soon as the bouncers let Coleman go, and before I could grab him, he swung at them; all the bouncers grabbed Coleman, picked him up, took him downstairs, and threw him on the gravel outside the club. They told him he couldn't come back in.

Coleman said, "Motherfucker, I will be back!"

I had forgotten that Coleman carried his gun everywhere. Coleman ran toward the car; I went back to get the homeboys and told them, "We are leaving."

As soon as we came back out of the club, Coleman had his gun, walking toward the club. Thank God we came out when we did. If we hadn't, Coleman would have started shooting. We took the gun from Coleman because we heard someone say, "They called the police." We put Coleman in the car and took off out of the parking lot back to Durham. I was so afraid because I just knew someone had taken our tag number and informed the police.

When we arrived in Durham, we stopped by Hardee's restaurant and ordered some food to take back to the apartment.

I could tell Coleman was still drunk because he had that glaze in his eyes. We ate our food and Coleman went to bed. The rest of us stayed up a little while to talk about what had happened, and then we went to bed. The next morning, Coleman didn't remember anything.

CHAPTER 32

God Was Warning Me

In the last two years of college, there was too much going on in my life. Trouble was following me everywhere I went. When I returned to Kinston to visit and go to the clubs, someone would always pick a fight. I was never a person that started trouble, but I didn't back down from anything. I had to take a step back and try to figure out what was going on. Was I hanging around the wrong crowd, or was I in the wrong place at the wrong time?

The friends I had weren't the fighting type, nor did they ever start trouble. I began to notice what was going on, but I couldn't put my finger on it. I knew something bad was going to happen to me, but I didn't know what. One night, I had this dream that I was riding in my classic—that's what I called my 1965 Buick convertible. In my dream, I wrecked the car and dreamed that I was paralyzed. When it came time for my college graduation, I wasn't able to walk across that stage.

This dream took place amidst all the troubles I was encountering, which was out of character for me. There were so many troublesome incidents I experienced in college that I can't recount them all, but an alarm should have gone off in my head during this one incident.

By then, Coleman and I had another roommate, who was also a close friend of mine. Basically, he was like a brother to me. Coleman never really liked him, but this brother would give you the shirt off his back. He and Coleman stayed in the same Parkview Apartments back in the 70s. Coleman didn't want him to stay there, but as I said before, our families were tight from living in Carver Courts together, plus he was a Jones.

Coleman made a comment to him, "The only reason you are staying here is because of Goldwater. Let's get this straight: I don't want you here, but Goldwater does. As long as you come up with your share of the rent each month, this won't be a problem, and you and Goldwater will be sharing rooms."

My friend Hook was free-hearted, a little too free-hearted at times. If a stranger walked by, he would welcome them into our house and invite them to our food and drinks. I remember walking into the house one day and seeing a guy I didn't know drinking a Budweiser. I didn't think anything of it; I just spoke and went about my business.

Later, when Coleman got off work, he went to the refrigerator for a beer and said, "Gold, did you drink my beer?" Of course, he didn't mind if I drank it; he would just go buy another six-pack. He said, "I know Hook doesn't drink, so who drank my beer?"

Hook told Coleman, "A friend came over, so I offered him a beer."

"Don't offer anybody my stuff! You can offer people your stuff in this house, but don't you ever give anyone none of what belongs to me unless I said they could have it!"

The same thing would happen to me when I came to the apartment, went into the closet, and found most of my liquor gone. The people in the neighborhood knew Hook was free-hearted, so they would come around just to get high. One day, I got a call from one of my homeboys asking me to pick him up from Raleigh/Durham Airport, like I said earlier, our apartment was where everyone stayed if they were visiting.

I used to pick up a guy named Wayne from the airport all the time; he might stay two or three days, or he might stay a week. Most of the time, I would go to Kinston for the weekend, so I wasn't there much. Wayne had just flown in from New York to Raleigh/Durham. Every time I picked him up, he would fill my tank up. He was my father's age, but he called himself raising me too.

One night, Wayne and Hook were talking in the living room, and it was getting late, so I decided to go to bed. I woke up about an hour later, and Wayne and Hook were still talking. I went to use the bathroom, and when I came out, I noticed their eyes were glossy. When I went into the kitchen, I saw a huge scale, one a person would see in science class, and I saw enough cocaine to get everyone in Durham high. I went back to sleep.

I didn't say anything, but I thought to myself, 'I know this guy isn't selling this stuff, and I know he didn't have this when I picked him up from the airport. I'm sure he didn't have it with him.' As I said before, my homeboys did their best not to let me see them do anything. They'd smoke a joint, sure, but everything else, no.

I fell back asleep for another two hours and remember someone coming into my room and turning on the light. It's hard for me to sleep with the light on. When I opened my eyes, they weren't fully focused, but I saw Wayne holding a gun, with Hook telling him everything was alright. Wayne had come into my room and turned over some clothes. I got up and wanted to know what the hell was going on and why Wayne was waving his gun like he was looking for something.

He was my homeboy, so I wasn't worried about him shooting me. I walked into the living room and saw the furniture turned over and all the cabinets opened. Wayne said, "There were people in the house trying to kill us!"

It didn't take a genius to figure out that Wayne was hitting too much of his own stuff. Not only was he hitting his own stuff, but he started having flashbacks of Vietnam. Wayne came into the living room and started shouting, "Everyone duck, there's the enemy!"

I didn't see any enemies; me, Hook, and Wayne were the only ones in the house. I knew our neighbors heard what was going on, especially Arthur and his brother next door; their last name was also Jones. As I mentioned earlier, when Coleman and I moved in, Coleman said, "Damn, the apartment next door is where we used to stay in the 70s."

As I said earlier, I knew Wayne wasn't going to hurt us, but he kept seeing people in the house, and I kept saying there wasn't anyone there. If they were, the closet was too small for them to hide in. It was hard to talk to Wayne with that gun waving around. He was a homeboy, and we couldn't just throw him out because his brother back in Kinston would have thought we did him wrong. It was fifteen degrees that night.

I told Hook, "You can take the classic and take Wayne back to Kinston, just make it back before class tomorrow." Wayne agreed to go back home. I remember Hook and Wayne getting into The Classic to go back to Kinston; Wayne still had the gun in his hand. I went back to my room and fell asleep. Thirty minutes later, Hook came back to the house.

"I know you didn't go to Kinston and come back that fast. Where's Wayne?"

"Gold, when we got by the Research Triangle area, Wayne made me get out of the car and open the hood because he said someone was in there. He also made me open the glove compartment because he thought someone was there. Gold, the way Wayne was waving that gun around, I was too damn nervous to drive."

It was ironic for Hook to use a curse word because I had never heard him curse before.

"Well, where is he?"

"I turned the car around and came back, and when I got on Fayetteville Street, Wayne told me to let him out."

"Hook, man, we got to find him because it's freezing outside."

"Wayne wanted to get out of the car and walk."

An hour later, I saw a lot of lights outside our door. I peeked out the curtains and saw a lot of police cars and the Special Weapons and Tactics Team (S.W.A.T.) going next door. I wanted to know, "What in the world is the S.W.A.T. Team doing at Arthur and his brother's home? They didn't do anything but work on cars. They didn't even drink."

After the S.W.A.T. Team left, I heard a knock on my window. When I looked out, it was Wayne.

"Open the door!"

I opened the door and asked, "Are you alright?" He said, "Yes."

I could tell he wasn't as high as he was before he left, but he still had the gun. He said he wanted to apologize to me and Hook; we couldn't go back to sleep. Wayne asked Hook if he could take him back to Kinston.

"You have to wait until I get out of class tomorrow." The next day, I saw Arthur and asked him why the S.W.A.T. Team was at their house last night. He said someone told the police that the Jones boys were being held hostage. Remember, I mentioned earlier that the guys who stayed next door were also Joneses.

"Give me more details," I said to Arthur.

He said, "The police knocked on the door and asked if the Jones boys stayed here. I told them, 'Me and my brothers' last name is Jones.' Then the police asked me if we were being held hostage, and I told them, 'No,' but they said they had to check the apartment out anyway."

The police said that some short fellow had stopped them last night and gave them our address, saying that the Jones boys were being held hostage. I turned around and looked at Wayne, who had a weird look on his face. I asked Wayne, "Did you send the police to our neighbor's apartment?"

"Yes."

Wayne's mind had gone back to the 70s to that same apartment where they had lived. I realized that me and Hook were the Jones boys Wayne told the police about. He had given them the apartment number of Arthur and that set of Joneses.

I was so pissed off, yet relieved at the same time, because if the police had come to my and Hook's apartment and asked if we were being held hostage, we would have said no. When the police had told us they had to check the apartment, they would have found enough cocaine to get everyone in Durham high, and also a scale big enough to weigh an animal.

We would have gone to jail for a long time for something we knew nothing about. Let me take that back: I would have gone to jail for something I didn't have anything to do with. Even if Wayne and Hook had taken the blame and told the police I didn't have anything to do with the drugs, the police wouldn't believe them. I'd still be in prison now if this incident had occurred. The police would have charged me with conspiracy because the drugs were at the house.

"Take Wayne back to Kinston."

This wasn't the first time Wayne had done something like that. I remember when I wasn't in town for the weekend; Wayne came from New York again, but Hook picked him up from the airport. They started getting high, and Wayne told Hook to close the curtains because the police were in the trees. Hook tried to convince him that there was no one in the trees. Wayne got his gun and shot up into the ceiling; just so happened our mother away from home, Aretha, was in the bathroom at the time, and a bullet came through the ceiling, missing her by a couple of inches.

Aretha came downstairs to see what was going on; she and Hook had to convince Wayne that there weren't any policemen in the trees. Aretha had a long talk with Wayne about getting himself together because things were getting out of hand with him. Aretha loved all of us from Kinston. Wayne promised he would get himself together.

Little did I know, Wayne was going back and forth to New York to pick up drugs. I'm glad I didn't know because I would have felt very uncomfortable around him. I still wasn't getting the message God was trying to convey to me; he was warning me that something was going to happen, but I just wasn't getting it. There were more things that happened before I understood the message. It was too late because I suffered for not heeding God's warning.

CHAPTER 33

My Friend Stephon Killed His Girlfriend

While attending North Carolina Central University, I met a friend named Stephon. Stephon had skin darker than midnight and a stature reminiscent of Arnold Schwarzenegger. He drove a Sentra and had a quiet, cool demeanor. He never messed with anyone. There was a time I thought he played for the North Carolina Central University football team, but after talking with him, he cleared that up—he wasn't on the team. He told me he had transferred from East Carolina University. I didn't know much about Stephon, but I remember someone saying he had to sit out a semester because, when he'd gone home for spring break and while at a party one night, someone slipped something into his drink that made him do weird things.

Once Stephon got himself together, he came back to school. I believe this incident happened before I arrived at North Carolina

Central University. I can't say if what people claimed happened to him is true or not, but I had heard that he used to burn Bibles behind his apartment. Nevertheless, that was the story on Stephon. Around me, he never exhibited any of the rumors I'd heard; he was one of the nicest guys I had ever met.

One Monday evening, Stephon and his girlfriend came by the apartment looking for my roommate—my roommate was selling weed at the time. Stephon asked if I could sell him some, and I told him he'd have to wait for my roommate to get back. My roommate didn't want me to see him selling weed because he knew my family and knew they wouldn't stand for that kind of activity around me. But my thought was, what he did was his business.

Anyway, when I came out of the room, I spoke to Stephon and his girlfriend. Stephon asked me, "What are you getting ready to do?"

"I have a class from 7 p.m. to 9:30 p.m."

"Come over to my apartment to see the game after class."

"I'll stop by."

I remember it as if it were yesterday because Stephon was a Cowboys fan, and the Cowboys were playing the St. Louis Cardinals for Monday Night Football. Stephon didn't drink, but I told him I'd bring a six-pack of Budweiser over for the game.

At 8:45 p.m., I slipped out of class, went to the store to buy the beer, and headed to Stephon's apartment. Just as I was arriving, the place was surrounded by detective cars—the Durham County police were there; there was a crime scene marked off with yellow tape.

I proceeded to go to the apartment with my beer. I remember saying out loud, "That looks like Stephon's apartment." The TV crew came over to me and asked, "Do you know this guy, Stephon?"

"Yes." The police wanted to talk to me, but the TV crew wanted to get their information first.

"How do you know him?"

"Because he is a friend of mine; I came over to watch football." I wasn't looking directly into the camera while talking; my mind was racing with what had happened. I remember the TV crew asking, "What type of guy was he?"

"He is a nice guy."

"Did he have a girlfriend?"

"Yes."

They were asking me all those questions because a girl had been found behind the apartment with about forty stab wounds, and they didn't know who she was. The police came over to talk with me because they weren't sure whether I might have had something to do with the crime or if I knew what went on. They were being slick with their questions, while I was being truthful with my answers. The police still wouldn't tell me what happened, and now that I think about it, they didn't want to give me any information just in case I was a possible accomplice in the crime.

One of the bystanders came over after the police had stopped questioning me and said, "I heard someone hollering, so I came out of the apartment and saw Stephon with no clothes on, running from the apartment. Stephon had stopped a lady at the traffic light, snatched her out of her car, and took off down the highway. When the police stopped the car, he got out, and I guess the police tried to rush him, and he broke one of the policeman's collarbones. From what I saw on the news, he was on the trunk of the car, naked, and the police had to rope him as if he were a beast to get him under control."

Later in my life, after graduating from college and starting my career, I was working at the Triangle Correctional Center in Raleigh, N.C., while Stephon was at Central Prison. For some strange reason when I found out Stephon was doing time at Central Prison, I sent word through someone to ask him if he remembered me. They said he did, but just barely.

When Stephon awakened the morning after his arrest, I understood that he could not remember committing the murder.

I often wonder if I could have prevented what happened if I had gotten out of class a little earlier or whether I would have been Stephon's victim, or if Stephon would have been mine.

Was this another warning from God? Was God still trying to speak to me? These are questions that will linger in my mind and remain in the back of my consciousness for the rest of my life. Was God trying to save me?

Though I don't know where Stephon is now, I hope God has given Jean's family the peace to close this painful chapter of their lives.

CHAPTER 34

God's Warning Came to Fruition

Earlier, I mentioned that I had a dream about being in a terrible car accident. I dreamed I had gotten in a car accident in that blue convertible. I was laid up in the hospital, paralyzed. The only thing on my mind was that I wasn't going to march with my class. I only had a few more weeks until my college graduation.

During the week of March 9, 1986, my college was out for spring break; this was my last year of college. I was scheduled to graduate on time (meaning in four years). When I arrived in Kinston, North Carolina, I went to spend time with my girlfriend and my daughter, who was nine months old. I kept her that week because my girlfriend was also attending college at Lenoir Community College.

A couple of days after I came home for spring break, I got sick and went to the emergency room because I had a high fever and chills. The doctors diagnosed me with a stomach virus. I improved as the week went by. My friend Capp was also home on spring break from Fayetteville State University. Another friend was visiting from Germany because his father had passed away.

It had been a long time since Junious, Capp, and the rest of the crew had all been home at the same time. The guys and I went to the barber shop to get haircuts. One of my friends who was cutting hair asked if we were going to the Chic Disco Tech later that night. The Chic was a popular disco in my hometown. For the previous nine weeks, the Chic had been giving away $100 for the talent show contest, and the winner advanced to the final round. This particular weekend, the Chic was going to pick the winner for the final contest and give away $1,000. My friend who was a barber was in the contest, and everyone felt he was going to win. While I was at the barber shop, he asked us to come out and cheer for him, and the guys said, "Sure, we're coming."

I knew I hadn't spent a lot of time with my girlfriend and child during spring break, so I was trying to figure out how to tell my girlfriend I was going out with the guys that night. After leaving the barber shop, we agreed to get back together later on. I went to my grandmother's house and started watching basketball; it was March Madness, and I think it was the final four weekend. Later, I went over to my girlfriend's apartment to spend time with them. Guilt washed over me about going out to party that night because I hadn't spent enough time with my girlfriend and children. Something inside me was saying, "Don't go," and "If the guys don't call, don't you call." But at the same time, my mind was saying, "Man, you're graduating in seven weeks, and then you can spend all the time you want with your girl and kids."

Junious called and said, "I'll be coming to pick you up around 10 p.m." I told my girlfriend that I was going out for about two hours because I had to leave to go back to college the next day. When Junious arrived to pick me up, I had that look on my face with guilt in my heart about going out, knowing I hadn't spent time with my family.

Junious and I arrived at Capp's place, but he said he wasn't ready and would meet us at the club later. We called Antray, who also said he'd meet us there. When Junious and I arrived at the club and went inside, my cousin Eric came over and asked me what I was drinking. I think I told him to get me a Private Stock beer. Jimmy came over and asked me what time I was leaving to go back on Sunday and if he could catch a ride. I told him, "Yes."

Junious, his girlfriend, and I were just chilling, waiting for the crew to arrive at the club. The DJ announced that the talent competition would start in ten minutes, so most of the crowd headed to the front of the stage. I remember Junious, his girlfriend, and I moving toward the stage when some guy came out of nowhere and put his hands on Junious's girlfriend's backside.

Junious and the guy got into an argument, and I stepped between them, telling Junious to drop it. The guy told me to stay out of it and said if I wanted, I could get some of the action. He even invited me outside to fight.

"I'm not going outside; if I'm going to fight you, it would be right now."

The guy kept trying to get me to leave the club, but I refused. For some reason, I didn't feel like fighting that night, plus I was dressed in a nice sport jacket, slacks, and my Pierre Cardin leather boots. I was too clean.

The guy called me a punk-ass motherfucker because I wouldn't go outside. I couldn't believe I was taking this kind of verbal abuse; if someone had disrespected me any other time, it would have been on.

After the guy couldn't convince me to go outside, I proceeded to get closer to the stage to watch the talent show. Five minutes later, someone hit me in the back of the head with their fist, and when I turned around, it was the same guy from earlier.

I hit him about five times before I picked him up over my head, body-slammed him onto the table, and began to whip his ass. He managed to bust my lip while he was down, and that's when I put my knees on each of his arms so he couldn't swing anymore. I just started beating the hell out of him. The next thing I knew, someone was pulling me off him and handing him a gun at the same time.

At first, I didn't see the gun until he pointed it at my face and shot twice, but the gun misfired. I managed to turn away just as something hit me in my right hip and butt area; all of a sudden, my whole right side went numb.

I was trying to get away when the guy shot me in the left hip, below my butt. Suddenly, I couldn't feel either leg and fell to the floor. The guy stood over me and shot toward my face, but he missed, and the gun jammed.

While I was lying on the floor, Antray rushed over and said, "Man, let's go! Someone has started shooting in here!"

"I'm the one who got shot."

"Stop playing. We've got to go!"

I kept insisting, "I'm the one who's been shot."

Antray wasn't convinced, so I pulled my pants down slightly to show him the blood. I could tell I was going into shock because I started getting cotton mouth.

My cousin Eric came over with the beer he said he'd get for me earlier when I first arrived at the club. I hadn't been there twenty minutes before all of this drama unfolded.

"Give me the beer because I can feel my throat closing in; it's to the point where I'm about to choke. Call the ambulance!"

One of the club workers said they had already called.

"Call them again because the ambulance is taking too long." I told the guys, "I can't feel anything from the waist down; I need them to get me to the car first," and I drank the beer.

When my friends lifted me into the car, I remembered the top part of my body feeling cold.

"What are you waiting for?" I asked Antray.

"I'm waiting for the car to warm up, and I can't go anywhere because another car has us blocked in."

Then all of a sudden, I heard another gunshot.

I asked the guys to cover me, "I think this fool is coming back to finish me off," but he had already left the scene; the shot I heard was someone else shooting in the air.

"We need to go; I need to get medical attention. Back the car up, ride on the sidewalk, and get me the hell out of here!"

On our way to the hospital, we passed the ambulance. After arriving, the guys took me out of the car and inside the hospital. I saw a lot of people from the club there. My cousin Sharon Mason was crying.

The guys asked the nurse for a gurney to put me on. The nurse working asked, "Aren't you the same guy who was in here Monday with a stomach virus? What were you doing out in the streets?"

When the nurse wheeled me back where doctors took care of patients, my cousin Eric was acting like a madman, yelling, "I'm going to kill the sucker who shot my cousin!"

The nurse told him he had to leave, or she'd have to call the police. Eric refused to comply, and the police came and arrested him. The scene was growing chaotic at the hospital. The nurse asked another one of my friends, Roscoe, to leave the area, but he wouldn't go until my grandmother arrived.

Roscoe was a big weightlifting guy, and the police didn't bother him. Word had started spreading that I had gotten shot, and more people were coming to the hospital. Things were spiraling out of control. The nurse hooked me up to the IV, and one nurse shoved a tube down my nose. I yanked it out because I was choking. That nurse didn't use any tact.

Another nurse came over and said, "Garry, you are bleeding inside your stomach, and we have to put this tube down your throat." She added, "I'm going to take my time, and as I push the tube down your nose, I want you to swallow to make the procedure easier."

The second nurse made the process smoother; the first one had treated me like crap. On top of that, a doctor walked in and sarcastically asked, "What were you doing at the bar?"

"I wasn't at no damn bar. You're going to talk to me like you got some sense."

He replied, "I don't like to be called in late at night."

At that moment, I could have busted that joker in the head. I guess he felt like I made his job hard; he was frustrated because he was a specialist called in the middle of the night. The doctor ordered the nurse to put a long needle in my penis, and I asked, "What in the hell are you all going to do with me?" By this time, my grandmother had arrived at the hospital. When the nurse tried to put the needle down my penis, I started hollering and cursing, and my grandmother told me that I'd better shut that fuss and not curse again.

If the doctor had just told me what was going on, it would have been so much better. They were prepping me for surgery and for a cystoscopy because they detected a lot of blood in my stomach. When my girlfriend walked into the hospital, the first thing I asked was, "Who's home with the children?"

She told me her mother had come to the apartment to stay with them. She was trying to convince me that everything was going to be alright. I wasn't buying that crap. I couldn't feel anything from the waist down, and I was being prepped for a cystoscopy. The doctors were concerned the bullet might have hit my kidneys.

I kept saying, "I'm going to kill that guy who shot me!" My Uncle Jay kept telling me I couldn't say that because if something happened to the guy who shot me, they'd charge me with a crime—conspiracy.

The doctor said again, "You had no business at the bar; I can smell alcohol on your breath."

"I had a beer because my mouth got dry after I got shot."

The hospital staff wheeled me to the operating room for exploratory surgery.

"Am I going to be paralyzed?"

"I don't know," the doctor said.

It appeared to me that the doctors didn't know a damn thing. I woke the next morning in a regular room. IVs were running everywhere, with tubes down my nose. I was in a complete mess, not knowing if I would ever walk again. All these nurses kept coming in dressed in green, and I was trying to figure out what was happening. Someone told me it was St. Patrick's Day.

The police were in my room asking questions about what happened; I couldn't provide much detail.

"Did you catch the guy?"

"No, but we know who he is because he shot two more people in the past."

The police said, "We spoke with the guy's friend who shot you; he told us it was all a setup and that you didn't start the fight. He said he and his buddy tried to get you to go outside with them, but when you didn't go, his buddy told him to hold the gun because he was going back inside to get you, and to only give him the gun if he was getting his ass kicked."

I guess if I had lost the fight, I would have never been shot. I suffered a long time after being shot, and I still suffer today because during the summer, my whole right side burns and in the winter, my right side aches. The bullet messed up my sciatic nerve. The good thing was that I wasn't paralyzed, and a week later, they took out the catheter and I could finally use the bathroom on my own! I was so glad!

That ordeal was an eye-opener! You see, when that gun didn't go off twice as the guy stood looking down at me while I looked up at him, I knew without a shadow of a doubt that there is a

God who looks out for fools and babies. I wasn't either of those that night, but I can honestly say He is a Good God, and I am grateful to be alive and well.

I think everybody that night was in rare form after the incident; Eric going to jail for being too concerned for his cousin, or maybe the alcohol had gotten the best of him; Roscoe protecting me and the surroundings until my grandmother arrived, or was it part of the drama of my getting shot, as in "As the World Turns."

I went to Duke University Hospital for surgery to remove the bullet and had several minor operations to ease the pain.

While in the hospital, I continued my studies to graduate. Two of my classmates, Janice Goodman and Loretta Moye, would come by the room to retrieve my term paper and turn it in. Janice took my work to one of my drama classes and slid the paper under the door, but the teacher had already gone to the registrar's office and turned in the grades, never returning to the classroom. He didn't receive my term paper, so he gave me an "I"—incomplete.

I didn't need this class to graduate; it was just an elective. However, I couldn't get my diploma with an "I" on my record. The university tried to track the teacher down because they wanted to see me march since I had come so far, but they couldn't reach him until Monday—graduation was on that Saturday. When they finally contacted the teacher and he saw my term paper, he gave me a B. I picked up my diploma a few days later. My earlier dream had come true; I wasn't able to march with my class, but I wasn't paralyzed.

God was trying to get my attention, and I knew it, but I didn't know what to do. What could I have done?

CHAPTER 35

No Justice, No Peace

After I returned from Durham, North Carolina, my mindset shifted to seeking justice for the person who shot me. I was still in a lot of pain from the permanent nerve damage, so I decided to go back home and stay with my grandmother instead of at my girlfriend's house.

My daughter was ten months old, and she cried often, which was getting on my nerves. I needed peace of mind, and because I was in such pain, I didn't want to be around anyone I cared about since I was irritable. My grandmother had patience; she could deal with my mood swings. I was in so much pain every day that drinking didn't help, and the doctors took me off narcotics before I became addicted. I was told I would be in this condition for a long time. I almost lost my damn mind. One minute my entire right side, from waist down, was burning, and the next hour it was throbbing from so much pain. I was so desperate that I went to church and let the preacher put his hand on my leg to relieve it.

My friends used to come over to take me out of the house for some fresh air. One day I told them they could take my car, let the top down, and drive me around since I was walking with a cane.

It was the Fourth of July, and everyone was out riding around or grilling. I was in the backseat with my friend Antray and a fifth of Jim Beam.

"Pull over to the convenience store; I want a cold beer," I said.

As Junious pulled over, he saw the guy who shot me. I didn't know what he looked like since the fight in the club was dark.

"Junious, are you sure that's him?"

"You damn right I'm sure!"

Antray confirmed this was the guy who shot me.

I said, "Let's get his ass! You all get out, catch him, and bring him to me because I can't run!"

When the guy recognized I was in the car, he took off running.

"Chase him in my car! Drive on the sidewalk if you have to!" While Antray was chasing him, the guy ran through some projects and got away. I was pissed because I wanted revenge. The police and the trial were taking too long. He wasn't going to walk around Kinston after shooting me and think he could get away with hurting me. After he shot the other two guys, he strutted around as if he couldn't be touched, but I wasn't going to allow him to stroll in peace. I wanted to send the message that, "Every time you see me, you'll run, and eventually we're going to meet, and I'm going to beat the hell out of you just like I did that night."

On another occasion, my friends came over to take me riding, and we ended up at Southeast Park. The crowd usually hung out at Southeast for a few hours before going over to Holloway Park on Sundays. I sat in the car for a few minutes because so many people came over to check on me. One guy approached and said, "There is the guy who shot you; do you want me to take care of him?"

"No, I want to handle it myself. You can put your gun away; I want to take care of it man to man."

The guy recognized my car this time and bolted for Holloway Courts. Eventually, my boys and I headed to Holloway Courts, and when I saw him, I shouted from a distance, "Don't run!"

He pulled out his gun as if to say, "If you come closer, I'll shoot you again," then he took off running. That's what cowards do; they won't fight with their hands; they want to use a gun. I grew up fighting with my fists.

One of my friends, Roscoe, was at the club one night and saw the guy again. Roscoe knew him because they were stationed at Camp Lejeune Marine Base together in Jacksonville, North Carolina. The guy noticed Roscoe staring and went to tell the club owner that Roscoe was trying to start some trouble.

Roscoe wasn't trying to stir up anything; he was just sending the guy a message that, "You can't walk around Kinston in peace after shooting one of my friends and think you're going to get away with it, so you might as well prepare to get your ass kicked whenever you're in public."

The club owner called the police, and the guy left because Roscoe wasn't going anywhere. Roscoe was a bodybuilder and as strong as an ox; he didn't need a gun to fight anyone. He usually dismantled someone with his bare hands. If Roscoe or another friend named Andre said they were going to get you, you could count on it. You might as well go ahead and fight them and get it over with because they would track you down until they found you.

Ironic, isn't it? Andre was the one who stabbed Roscoe back in the day when we were growing up in Carver Courts.

The next week, it was time for me to go to trial and face the guy who shot me. The charges he faced included assault with a deadly weapon with intent to kill and inflicting serious bodily injuries. When we arrived in court, the guy never showed up. A warrant was issued for his arrest, but I learned that he picked up his paycheck the week before trial and never returned to work; he skipped town and went back to New York. I received no justice, and he is definitely not experiencing any peace.

It has been thirty years, and the police still haven't caught him. Will they ever catch him? Have they closed the case? Is the guy dead? I don't know. The only thing I do know is that two thoughts cross my mind regularly: "Will I forgive the guy, or will I seek revenge?" I will never know the answer to the question until I face the guy who shot me.

Epilogue

Growing up, when I used to hear people say, "People are a product of their own environment," it was used in a negative context. However, as I got older, I understood that we are all products of our environments, whether positive or negative. I saw more positivity growing up in Carver Courts, so I chose to emulate the positive influences I received from my family and community.

During my last year of college, on spring break, I suffered two gunshot wounds stemming from an altercation I tried to defuse. Ultimately, a fight ensued, the tides turned, and I became a survivor of gun violence. This incident never deterred me from making a positive impact in others' lives. Many people assumed that because I grew up in a housing project like Carver Courts, I was a product of my environment in a negative sense. I don't condone or glorify violence, but in reality, God left me here for a purpose, and hopefully, one day, I will discover that purpose and work to fulfill it.

Where Are They Now

Front Row Left to Right, Uncle John Jones, Grandmother Tessie Jones and Uncle Earl Jones Second Row Left to Right, Cousin Annie Mae Grimes, Aunt Mamie Jean Johnson, Denderant Jones, Aunt Arnetta Dixon, Mother Vergie Chalmers, Aunt Mary Mason, and Aunt Mavis Jones

John Wesley Jones: Retired Principal from Lenoir County Public Schools – 36 Years

Tessie Simmons Jones:
Domestic Work (Deceased)

Earl Kenlaw Jones:
25 Years at Manufacturing Plant (Deceased)

Annie Grimes Burt:
32 Years of Government Services to Present

Mamie Jones Johnson
Retired from Government Services – 37 Years ((Deceased)

Denderant Jones Burney:
30 Plus Years with Educational System (Deceased)

Arnetta Jones Dixon:
37 Years of Government Services (Deceased)

Vergie Jones Chalmers:
20 Years of Government Services

Mary Jones Mason:
Retired from Government Services 30 Plus Years (Deceased)

Mavis Colleen Jones:
42 Years of Government Services (Retired)

All First Male Cousins – First Row, Left to Right, Terry (PePe Jones) Larry (L.B.) Burney Jr. Second Row, Jerome Jones, Curtis (Blow) Johnson, Brian (Ross) Johnson, Garry (Goldwater) Jones, Garrick (G.) Dixon, Cedric Dixon and Carlos Hardy.

Left to Right Pete, Lisa and of Course Me

My Grandmother, Tessie Jones and Me When I Was a Little Boy

My Grandfather, Wesley Jones (Deceased)
My Father's Side of the Family

First Row: My Grandmother Frances Dove & My Grandfather
Milton Dove Sr. (Deceased) Second Row:
My Aunt Timber Washington,
My Aunt Kaye Jackson, My Aunt Lorna Dove,
My Aunt Velma Dove & My Father Milton Dove Jr.

My Father Now

Left to Right: My Brother Duane King,
My Father Milton Dove Jr., My Sister Kayla Dove &
My Sister Alicia Rooks

www.ingramcontent.com/pod-product-compliance
Lightning Source LLC
Chambersburg PA
CBHW021144080526
44588CB00008B/216